Recovery:

A Return
To The Self

By
Donna Kasik

Editorial Assistance By
Joshua Collins

Recovery: A Return to the Self

Copyright © 2010 by Donna Kasik

    Library of Congress Control Number: 2010931070
    Kasik, Donna, 1961--
    Recovery: A Return to the Self

ISBN 978-1-935434-51-1
Subject Codes and Description: 1. REL 012120
Religion: Christian Life - Spiritual Growth;
2. SEL 021000 Self-Help: Motivation and Inspiriation;
3. SEL 029000 Self-Help - Twelve Step Programs.

All rights reserved, including the right to reproduce this book or any part thereof in any form, except for inclusion of brief quotations in a review, without the written permission of the author and GlobalEdAdvance Press.

Cover Design by Barton Green

The Press does not have ownership of the contents of a book; this is the author's work and the author owns the copyright. All theory, concepts, constructs, and perspectives are those of the author and not necessarily the Press. They are presented for open and free discussion of the issues involved. All comments and feedback should be directed to the Email: comments4author@aol.com and they will be forwarded to the author for response.

    Printed in the United States of America

Published by
GreenWine Family Books™
A division of GlobalEdAdvancePress

www.globaledadvance.org

Dedication

This book is dedicated to my son, a voracious reader of Scripture, who helped me to see that the Bible is the only path to understanding, and how little everything else in life matters in comparison.

> *"I regard everything as loss because of the surpassing value of knowing Christ Jesus my Lord. For His sake I have suffered the loss of all things, and I regard them as rubbish, in order that I may gain Christ and be found in Him, not having a righteousness of my own that comes from the law, but one that comes through faith in Christ, the righteousness from God based on faith. I want to know Christ and the power of His resurrection and the sharing of His sufferings by becoming like Him in His death... forgetting what lies behind and straining forward to what lies ahead, I press on toward the goal for the prize of the heavenly call of God in Christ Jesus."*
>
> **Philippians 3:8-10 & 13b-14**

TABLE OF CONTENTS

Foreword:
The Graceful Journey & the Blueprint   **9**

Introduction:
Wandering the Wilderness   **17**

PRINCIPLES:

Chapter One:
The Blindness of Being Lost   **31**

Chapter Two:
The Deceptions in Life   **55**

Chapter Three:
Defining the Terms   **69**

Chapter Four:
The Grace of God   **83**

PRACTICE:

Chapter Five:
The Road to Recovery   **105**

Chapter Six:
The Wisdom of the Dying   **129**

Conclusion:
The Process of Recovery   **155**

References   **161**

"Blessed are those who hunger and thirst for righteousness, for they will be filled."

(Matthew 5:6)

FOREWORD

The Graceful Journey & the Blueprint

A Simple Statement

I live with the knowledge that God is good and that He loves us; this statement may sound simple, but without the knowledge of it, I would have been crushed into powder a long time ago. I say that God is good and that He loves us with a deep faith and assurance that, through all of the trials and tribulations that life brings, I have "the peace of God, which surpasses all understanding" (Philippians 4:7) and I realize that, "...we know that all things work together for good for those who love God and are called according to His purpose" (Romans 8:28). Having a Heavenly Father who loves us and walks life's journey with us enables us to confront ourselves for who we are and to recover (or perhaps to discover) who we were meant to be, which is a realization many of us have lost along the way.

The book you are reading is entitled, "Recovery: A Return to the Self." What does it mean to "return to the self?"— It means that we were originally created to walk with God and to follow His principles, as illustrated in Scripture. The "return to the self" is a recovery; it is a recovery of who we were meant to be that was lost in our original separation from God through the first sin and in our continued separation from Him in our ignorance and apathy regarding God's love for us. To return to the self is *to recover the self* — the self who God intended from the beginning, not the self we have clumsily crafted with our own errant hands. We can have a powerful, life-changing transformation in Christ when we believe in Him, when we trust in Him, and when we give our lives to Him. After this initial transformation, we can then get to know Christ more and more and learn how to be a Christ-follower through the Truth of Scripture (that we should read on a daily basis). Through the Bible, we should be trying to return to the intentions of God, i.e. to recover God's initial design for our lives, that is, to recover ourselves. In order to illustrate the "recovery" and "return" I speak of, this book is written in two main sections: Principles (Chapters 1-4) and Practice (Chapters 5-6). Chapters 1-4 provide the principles that lead to recovery, and Chapters 5-6 demonstrate how they work in real-life situations.

God, through His amazing grace and mercy, brought people into my life to make such a journey of recovery possible and to teach me many truths I would not have discovered on my own. Some of the people who have taught me the most are my Hospice patients and their families, care-givers, and friends. Unfortunately, many people do not return to themselves (that is, return to who they were meant to be) until their final months of life. It is often in those last months that people discover what they should have known all along: there is a map to life, but many do not read it. What is this map? — It is the Bible, a Blueprint for life, which I often read in the quiet homes of the dying. It is only in dying to ourselves that we ever really live, and it is in the Bible where we see the Truth that brings life.

Blueprints in Construction
Jesus worked as a carpenter, and one thing carpenters need to know is how to read a plan, a blueprint. Without a blueprint,

a worker has no idea where to begin, let alone what the final structure is supposed to look like, or how to get there. I was a construction painter in Chicago for many years before I became a chaplain. One of the buildings I painted, in Chicago, was the largest concrete structure in the world. My foreman and I were supposed to block-fill the cinder block in one of the many sub-basements of this huge building. My foreman could not find the blueprint, but he was trying to remember where the rooms were that we needed to work on, so we headed in the right direction, did the best we could, found a large room that we assumed was the right room, and crawled in. I say "crawled," literally, as the room had a small opening that we could not fit our ladders into; we could only crawl through with our tools and paint buckets. Once we crawled through the tiny opening, we found that the room was huge and almost impossible to paint. The ceiling of this sub-basement room was about thirty feet high, and we were unable to use a ladder or scaffolding since we could not get either piece of equipment through the small doorway.

Block filler is a thick latex paint that is applied with a large, fat, heavy roller-sleeve in order to fill the holes of cinder block prior to painting. Applying block filler is physically difficult work since the painter has to push onto the roller with a lot of force in order to fill all the holes in the block. Without a ladder or scaffolding, we were forced to extend our rolling poles to their maximum length, which was about twenty feet, and then press onto the blocks in order to fill in the holes. We could not get close to the walls either since there was a large, deep chasm between where we stood and the walls that needed the block filler. We were sweating within minutes, and our shoulders, backs, and arms were wearying as we rolled out the block filler onto the walls. I was practically in tears as we did this laborious work for hours. I wanted to quit with each stroke. We had to take quite a few breaks in order to keep our strength up to finish the room. Finally, exhausted and sore, we finished, crawled out of the hole, and went home.

The next day, my foreman asked how I was feeling, and I said, "Still sore and exhausted! I am dreading today, since we have to go back and paint that room!" He half-laughed while he looked slightly guilty; then he said, "Oh, don't worry; we block-filled the wrong room! I found the blueprint, and we were a room off." The room that needed to be block-filled was a small room, with a large doorway that would easily accommodate a six-foot ladder, which is all that was needed. We painfully exerted ourselves, worked incredibly hard, sweated profusely, strained practically every muscle in our bodies, and suffered pain for days for nothing — because we did not have the blueprint. We just guessed, assumed we were correct since we had both painted for a long time and knew the building well, and we did the best we could. Unfortunately, we failed miserably, wasted time, and hurt ourselves unnecessarily. We assumed, in our knowledge, in our experience, and in our arrogance, that we knew what we were doing. We did what was right in our own eyes, even though it turned out to be wrong. Time, money, and a great deal of energy were wasted, which resulted in a lot of pain, simply because we failed to read the blueprint. In our ignorance, we could not even walk into the room we mistakenly block-filled, but like the serpent in Genesis 3, with his lies and deception, we were forced to crawl into that large room. As is often true in life, without looking at the blueprint, we did not even know where to begin. I learned a spiritual lesson through this experience. I learned just how much time and energy is wasted, and how much unnecessary pain we go through in life, because we fail to read the Blueprint.

Listen carefully to those around you. Pay attention to circumstances, people, problems, and most of all, listen to God as you walk your own paths and possibly recover the self you too may have lost along the way by avoiding Scripture.

God still speaks to us today through His Word. Awareness is crucial. From even before we were born, God had a beautiful plan for each of our lives, tailor-made to fit our unique personalities. Yet, many never reach their full potential or live the lives God intended for them since many never learned what was expected from them. There is only one place where we can discover ultimate Truth and who we are meant to be: the Bible, the Word of God. I ask you to listen to God in the still, small voice found in Scripture. Ask God to transform you totally as He becomes the Lord of your life. Surround yourself with people who have had the experience of new life, and learn about how to live this life through the wisdom of the Bible. God speaks with marvelous love throughout each page, and He gives us, in His Word, the Blueprint for life, and life abundantly, so that we may truly live.

I am indebted to all the people who have graced my life through the past several years during the many transitions therein; some of these people have caused me great heartaches, and some have granted me great joys. However, all of these people have taught me that it is never too late to recover myself through the power of God's Word by living in His intimate presence.

> **"Before I formed you in the womb I knew you."**
> **(Jeremiah 1:5)**

Principles

"Know therefore that the Lord your God is God; he is the faithful God, keeping his covenant of love to a thousand generations of those who love him and keep his commands."
(Deuteronomy 7:9)

INTRODUCTION

Wandering the Wilderness

Caution:
The Words of God Through The Teachings of Jesus Can Offend

"I know what you are doing: you are neither cold nor hot. How I wish you were either one or the other! So, because you are lukewarm, neither cold nor hot, I will vomit you out of my mouth! For you keep saying, 'I am rich, I have gotten rich, I don't need a thing! You don't know that you are the one who is wretched, pitiable, poor, blind, and naked!" (Revelation 3:14-16). What does this passage mean? To whom is God speaking? Specifically, God is speaking to the church in Sardis. Did I say the CHURCH? — Yes! God is referring to the complacent "Christian" who is content simply living his/her life as a "good" person, who goes to church on Sunday, who puts a little money in the offering plate each week, who says grace before meals, who is kind and helpful, but who never fully surrenders to the Lordship of Christ, though he/she tries to absorb His love, mercy and grace, without the sacrifice God requires. After all, Jesus died for us, and all we have to do is believe, right? — Wrong; that is the description of one who is lukewarm, who actually nauseates God to the point of being vomited out of His mouth. None of us think we actually nauseate God, unless maybe we are in some terrible sin, but surely not as we are living our "good" lives. Oh, we can be so blind! Thankfully, the passage quoted above goes on to say, "I counsel you to buy from Me gold refined in the fire, so you can become rich; and white clothes to wear, so you can cover your shameful nakedness; and salve to put on your eyes, so you can see," (Revelation 3: 18).

There are far too many lukewarm "Christians" living unfulfilled, chaotic lives; I know this to be true; I struggled as one. I see lukewarm Christians all the time. I know "lukewarmness" all too well. I write this book through personal experience, through losing myself along the way in life by not reading the Bible (and therefore not following the Word of God), and through a continued daily struggle that will remain until I die. The words of the book you are reading are written both to you and to me as a constant reminder to read the Scriptures daily in order to know who God is, what God expects from us, and how to live out the Christian life.

Losing Ourselves
Some people expect the Christian life to be easy, but Jesus never promised His followers that their lives would be free of pain and suffering. Jesus actually said, "In this world you *will* have persecution. But take courage; I have overcome the world" (John 16:33B, italics mine). Christ-followers should enter Heaven bruised, battered, bloody, and exhausted, but also filled with wonder, hope, and unspeakable joy, knowing they lived their lives trying to fulfill the call God placed upon them. Following Jesus is not easy; He never said it would be. Rather, Jesus told us to count the cost: "For which of you, intending to build a tower, does not first sit down and estimate the cost, to see whether he has enough to complete it?... So therefore, none of you can become my disciple if you do not give up all of your possessions" (Luke 14: 28 & 33). I

believe that in context, through other passages in the Bible, that "possessions" can also refer to "desires," or anything that we hold dear. Count the cost before calling yourself a Christian, for it is quite high. It demands your entire life. Jesus also said, "If any want to become my followers, let them deny themselves and take up their cross and follow me. For those who want to save their life will lose it, and those who lose their life for my sake, and for the sake of the gospel, will save it. For what will it profit them to gain the whole world and forfeit their life?" (Mark 8:34-36).

Giving up your entire life to God is the most rewarding life imaginable since Jesus promises us His peace, His joy, and His abiding presence. All of these promises are written throughout Scripture. God said, "I will never leave you or forsake you" (Hebrews 13:5 and Joshua 1:5). Paul wrote in Philippians 4:7, "And the peace of God, which surpasses all understanding, will guard your hearts and your minds in Christ Jesus." Jesus said, "I came to give you life, and have it abundantly" (John 10:10). Unfortunately, many of us never find the peace and abundant life that God promises us. Why? Why do so many "Christians" live in confusion, chaos, brokenness, and pain? Why do so many "Christians" never know the joy of the Lord or live in the power of His love, but instead live in sins and addictions that they cannot seem to conquer, and are directionless, almost hopeless? — Because they do not know the power of God's Word, they have not had a life-changing experience through Christ, and they do not read Scripture to learn to live in this new life. Such "Christians" do not therefore even know God, since they have no idea what He says, what He does, how He works and what He has to offer them. They have no idea that there is an actual Blueprint for life that helps them navigate through life's storms and uncertainties and that can help them avoid many troubles and pains. There is a Blueprint that gives a picture of God so that we can know Him; this Blueprint is the Bible.

Opinion vs. Fact

If we call ourselves Christians, then we need to know the answers to questions regarding what Christ taught, why He came to earth, how He fulfilled the Old Testament, to what the New Testament is referring, and what the Christian faith is actually about; the only way these questions are answered is through the Bible. If I say, "I am a Christian," then I need to know the Bible; this concept is no different than if I say, "I am a mechanic" — I need to know about cars and how engines work. You may call yourself a Christian because you go to church and know some basic Bible stories, but surely this is not the extent of Christianity, nor is this the definition of a "Christian." The Christian faith is not a matter of opinion, but a matter of fact. A Christian is a Christ-follower, plain and simple. Does Jesus define His followers? — He does indeed define what a Christian is, what a Christian looks like, and how a Christian lives life. Jesus' definition is vastly different from most of ours. We find His definition in Scripture. However, if we do not read the Bible, then we, of course, have no way of understanding.

Following Jesus is the most satisfying and fulfilling path in life to take, and is the path intended for all of us, for our own benefit. The Christian walk is the path to recovery from the messes many of us have made of our lives. Many of us have lost ourselves by giving up and giving in to the false teachings of various churches due to Scriptural ignorance. When Christian churches do not study the Word of God (but teach human tradition instead of Godly Truth), and those in the pews do not read and study the Bible, false doctrines are perpetuated, shallow lives are lived, and lukewarm Christians are born. Such "Christians" live with no direction or strength, and are tossed all over the darkened corners of ignorance and apathy. Lukewarm Christians fail in their religion as they live in confusion and uncertainty; they give up on God as they lose themselves to spiritual defeat. Many have become addicted to ignorance because they have no idea what the Faith they profess to follow actually is, and they live fragmented lives in search of a Truth many feel they cannot ever find. We need recovery. We need a basic return to the Truth of God as found in the Bible. We need to be the people He created us to be. We need a "return to the self."

Simple Words of Wisdom
In my middle-aged years, I finally started down my own path to recovery. I discovered what Robert Frost called, "the Road less traveled," and I found it to be a road where I would not so easily get lost. I immersed myself in Scripture, and found the path where I knew God was with me — not because I imagined Him to be, but because I had endeavored to know Him through the means by which He commanded. I also began working as a hospice chaplain, which brought me to the bedside of the dying. I learned to be grateful that I was called into chaplaincy that I might glean from the dying what wisdom is often found when one stands on the threshold between life and death. While working as a hospice chaplain, I met a woman whose faith helped to direct me to this path; let's call her "Betty."

Betty was mentally-challenged and had never experienced life beyond the mountains of Eastern Kentucky. Despite her challenges, she provided excellent care for her husband, who was bed-ridden and dying of cancer. I used to visit Betty and her husband in their modest home in a "holler" in the Appalachian Mountains. What I remember most about her is that she was so proud to tell me that they owned two Bibles. Once, she asked if I would like to see her Bibles. She retrieved them from a shelf, and I asked if I could read from one. She smiled, as her face glowed, and replied, "Sure," as she took the other Bible to follow along with me. I began to read from one of my favorite Psalms:

"O Lord, you have searched me and know me,
You know when I sit down and when I rise up;
You discern my thoughts from far away.
You search out my path and my lying down,
And are acquainted with all my ways.
Even before a word is on my tongue,
O Lord, you know it completely.
You hem me in, behind and before,
And lay your hand upon me.
Such knowledge is too wonderful for me;
It is so high that I cannot attain it.
Where can I go from your spirit?
Or where can I flee from your Presence?
If I ascend to heaven, you are there;
if I make my bed in Sheol, you are there.
If I take the wings of the morning
And settle at the farthest limits of the sea,
Even there your hand shall lead me,
And your right hand shall hold me fast.
If I say, 'Surely the darkness shall cover me,
And the light around me become night,'
Even the darkness is not dark to you;
The night is as bright as the day,
For darkness is as light to you.

For it was you who formed my inward parts;
You knit me together in my mother's womb.
I praise you,
For I am fearfully and wonderfully made.
Wonderful are your works; that I know very well.
My frame was not hidden from You,
When I was being made in secret,
Intricately woven in the depths of the earth.
Your eyes beheld my unformed substance.
In your book were written all the days
That were formed for me,
When none of them as yet existed."

Psalm 139: 1-16

When I had finished reading, I closed the Bible, glanced up at Betty, and saw on her face a child-like light. She was absolutely beaming... touched by something in God's Word.

"Did you hear that?" asked Betty as she tapped her husband's arm. "She read from the Bible. Isn't that great?" Betty stared at me in wonderment.

I was, of course, surprised by her reaction. Never before had I seen anyone react that way to hearing the Bible read aloud. What exactly had moved her so overwhelmingly? Why did I not have a similar reaction when the Bible was read to me? All at once, the words of Jesus came into my mind: "... whoever does not receive the kingdom of God like a child will not enter it," (Mark 10: 15). Was I receiving God's Kingdom properly? — Betty sure seemed to be doing so. I did not know whether to laugh or to hide. Betty, in her genuine pleasure in hearing God's Word, had stripped me of my own affectations; she had become my teacher.

Living and Dying in Confusion
I have asked many dying people who profess to know Christ if they are assured of their salvation. To my amazement, many dying people have said "No," but they are merely "hoping" to go to Heaven. Scripture teaches otherwise. Scripture teaches that we can indeed have assurance of salvation. Others, who also told me they were Christian, said that they "think" they are going to Heaven because they have been good, kind people, they have never committed any horrible atrocities, and they have been church-members for many years. Scripture teaches otherwise. Scripture teaches that we cannot get to Heaven through our own merit, but only by the sacrifice Jesus made on our behalf on the cross; we need not only to believe in that atonement, but we need to live in that reality. The Bible tells us how our salvation is accomplished, but if we are unfamiliar with Scripture, then many will die in fear and uncertainty.

The conversations I have had with the dying concerning their fear of death, due to their Biblical ignorance, was one motivating factor that caused me to write this book. Another motivating factor was looking at the chaotic and sad lives so many people lead, and the pain they inflict on themselves and others because they live outside of the protective, loving boundaries of God, which are found in the Bible. We do not have to live and die in ignorance, uncertainty, or confusion. We have been given the Truth!

Far too many of us go through life basically lost. Many of us wander in wildernesses of our own makings. Many of us stumble around in the dark aimlessly. Many of us are confused. We often try to figure out what it is that we want, who we are, and what our purpose in this life may be, but we are blind and lost, and we do not even realize our blindness. We try to follow a faith we know nothing about. Some of us know there is something that is not quite right, but we are not sure what that "not quite right" thing is. I am convinced the "not quite right" thing is our ignorance of Scripture; it leads to a distance from God that was never meant to be. God originally walked closely with humanity. God talked to Adam and Eve, and He wanted an intimate relationship with them. Humans destroyed their intimate relationship with God back in the Garden of Eden when they rebelled against Him. Humanity has been rebelling ever since. People do not believe in the Word of God or even try to understand the words of Scripture, and therefore they do not have the transformational experience God intends for all people to have. Once we allow God to change our hearts, our minds, and our lives, we can learn who He is and what He wants for us and from us in the Bible. It is from our lack of reading the Bible, knowing its contents, and living in its Truth that we distance ourselves from God; in that distance from Him is where we lose ourselves.

Refusing to Read

Why is it that so many "Christians" do not read their Bibles? Why do some "Christians" take God's Word so lightly, and why do their Bibles sit in the car or on a shelf until Sunday when they might take it in to church? Why do so many people who believe they are Christians know only a little *about* God and yet do not actually *know Him*? A relationship is impossible without communication. It is impossible to know someone unless that person interacts with you, you listen to them, you hear them, you understand them, and you spend time with them. How do we cultivate a relationship with a Being like God? — By reading His Word so that we can hear His voice in the pages of the Bible. We can read about what God does and how He acts through the stories and teachings written in Scripture. God reveals His character through Scripture, but if we do not read it, we cannot know God. Can we know another human being without listening to him, without spending time with him, and without talking to him whom we can see and touch? — If not, then why do we think we can know God apart from His Word? Without God's Word, all we can know are things that others say about Him (which might be far from the truth). We would then miss the most wonderful thing on earth: actually knowing God personally and intimately, which is what He desires. Without intimately knowing God through Jesus Christ, we miss out on so much of life. If we do not read the Bible, then we are blind to the fact that we are actually lost and alone. We were created for God's pleasure, to be in relationship with Him, to know Him, to love Him, and to serve Him. If we refuse to read the Bible, then we are telling God that we are simply not interested in what He has to say, we do not want to hear Him, and we have better things to do than to listen to our Maker, the Creator of the universe, and our Savior for all eternity.

For some strange reason, many people (even those who call themselves Christians), think that they can go where they want, when they want, do what they want, and yet still believe they are on their way to Heaven; the Bible does not affirm such a false belief. Paul, the writer of most of the New Testament, called himself a "slave" or "bondservant" of Christ. Paul claimed to have no will of his own, but he did only what his Master told him to do. Jesus said the only people who can call themselves His followers are those who, "...deny themselves and take up their cross and follow Me" (Mark 8:34). Many Christians know Mark 8:34, but they do put this verse into practice. What does it mean to take up your cross? We do not practice crucifixion today, but in the days of Jesus, taking up your cross meant going to your death. We are told by Jesus that we must die to ourselves in order for Him to give us new life. He longs to give us new life.

Recovery
This book is about recovery... recovering our selves from false teachings, ignorance of Scripture and God's nature, apathy, and uncertainty. We can recover ourselves through a deep faith and understanding of Jesus Christ which can only come through the daily study of His Word and through the complete surrender of our lives to Him. We need more than the knowledge of God; "You believe God is one; you do well. Even the demons believe — and shudder" (James 2:19). "Christians" think they know God, apart from a deep, intimate, personal relationship with Jesus Christ — Impossible! Some "Christians" think they know God because they pray, they read their Bibles once in a while, they go to church most Sundays, they sit on some church board or they sing in the choir, but they are lukewarm. Jesus said, "If any want to become my followers, let them deny themselves and take up their cross daily and follow me" (Luke 9:23). Jesus also said, "Whoever comes to me and does not hate father and mother, wife and children, brothers and sisters, yes, and even life itself, cannot be my disciple" (Luke 14:26). Jesus did not mean literally to "hate" others, since He always commanded us to

love, and to love sacrificially. His strong language was used to emphasize that we should love Him above all else, and that, in comparison to Him, nothing else matters, as is explained in Matthew 10:37-39: "Whoever loves mother and father more than Me is not worthy of Me; and whoever loves son or daughter more than Me is not worthy of Me; and whoever does not take up the cross and follow Me is not worthy of Me. Those who find their life will lose it, and those who lose their life for My sake will find it." These are the radical words of Jesus — not mine; these words are how Jesus defines His followers. The "lukewarm" Christian will stand before Him on the Day of Judgment and may hear, "You that are accursed, depart from me into the eternal fire prepared for the devil and his angels" (Matthew 25:41). Notice that Hell was never intended for humans, but it was created for "the devil and his angels." God desires all people to love Him, to serve Him, and to be with Him in Heaven (2 Peter 3:9). We, not God, choose our eternal destiny. He gives us the freedom to love Him, and He never forces His love or our obedient response. Unfortunately, many will hear from the voice of God, "I never knew you," as recorded in the book of Mathew:

"Not everyone who says to me, 'Lord, Lord,' will enter the kingdom of heaven, but only the one who does the will of my father in heaven. On that day many will say to me, 'Lord, Lord, did we not prophesy in your name, and cast out demons in your name, and do many deeds of power in your name?' Then I will declare to them; 'I never knew you; go away from me, you evil-doers'" (Matthew 7:21-23).

How frightening! When children are lost, they are naturally frightened. However, as adults, many are lost, but do not have the good sense to be frightened. To do the will of God is to love Him, which we do when we follow Scripture. Jesus said, "If you love me, you will keep my commandments" (John 14:15). How can we keep God's commandments if we do not even know them? How can we know His commandments if we do not read the Bible?

None of us can have an intimate relationship with God through our own power, goodness, knowledge, or spirituality. None of us are quite "good" enough to have a close relationship with God. A friend of mine once said to me that we cannot all find recovery of ourselves in Jesus Christ because we cannot all live according to Scripture, pray without ceasing, and literally breathe and walk every moment with Him. "Not all of us can do that," he said. He was right, though not completely; NONE of us can do that on our own. Only God can enable us to have an intimate relationship with Him and to find recovery through the power of the Holy Spirit. Only God can place a desire in us for Him, since human nature is naturally rebellious and far from God. For those of us who desire to be Christians (Christ-followers), all we can do is open ourselves up to God and ask Him for the strength, the wisdom, and the ability to know Him. We cannot just know about Him, but we need to draw near to Him, as He promises to draw near to us (James 4:8). Then, we need to read His Word daily in order to get to know who God is and how a Christ-follower is defined by Christ Himself. However, be careful; if you draw near to God through His Word, you will experience a radical change!

Jesus followed the Old Testament Scriptures perfectly, which was a radical departure from the practices of the people of His day (including the religious elites). Jesus was radical. His teachings and His life were radical. He offended many. He commands us in Scripture to live a radically different life from what this world has to offer and from what our puny imaginations can conjure up. Jesus offers us "abundant" life (John 10). However, if we live in blindness, ignorance, and apathy towards Scripture, then we miss out on the "abundant" life. Do not wait to lie on your deathbed in order to discover the joy and unimaginable peace of a radical devotion to

Jesus Christ. We can have an intimate relationship with Jesus through the beauty of the greatest work of literature ever written — the Bible. Do not wait until your physical demise for spiritual recovery. Recovery can begin today.

My prayer is that you are somewhat offended and uncomfortable with this book. Jesus offended many people, which is why the "religious" elites of Christ's earthly days wanted to kill Him. Lukewarm, complacent "Christians" today can be compared to the "religious" elites of Christ's days. The Church today needs to be offended and awakened. May we all be awakened and offended together!

> **"Do not think that I have come to bring peace to the earth; I have not come to bring peace, but a sword. "**
>
> **— Jesus (Matthew 10:34)**

"The Lord opens the eyes of the blind."

(Psalm 146:8)

CHAPTER ONE

The Blindness of Being Lost

Blowing in the Wind
"Hey man, I like your bumper-sticker!" said my friend, who rolled down his window from the passenger's side of my van to convey his thoughts to the owner of the car parked next to us. My friend, who was laughing, asked if I saw the man's bumper- sticker.

"No," I said, I had not seen it.

It says, "How many roads must a man walk down before he admits he is lost?" We both laughed as we remembered the old Bob Dylan song, "Blowing in the Wind," that asks, "How many roads must a man walk down, before you can call him a man?" It was not until the next day that I really thought about that bumper sticker in a deeper way. How many roads have I walked down before I realized that I too was lost? — but what I had lost was myself. How do you lose yourself? — It is much easier than you may think; it is a spiritual loss that can be reclaimed only through the difficult and painful journey of confronting our humanity in all of its ignorance and returning to the Bible where the Blueprint for life is laid before us. Awareness through Jesus, whom we can know through

Scripture, brings recovery. Unfortunately, many of us do not take the time to learn to read the Bible (the Blueprint), so we do not get to know Jesus. However, God laid out His plans for us in His Word. All we need to do to live successfully is to read consistently, to learn, and to obey.

Far too often, people do not walk the spiritual journey that enables them to recover themselves until their lives are almost over. Many of us are so busy living that we often forget we are also dying. Perhaps I think of death more than the average person since I work for Hospice, where almost all of our patients are going to die within six months. Death is never a distant, surreal concept, but it is merely a natural reality of life. As a chaplain, I did not begin to recover myself until I had the opportunity to sit with the dying, their families, and their friends. I realized that in the business and difficulties of life, we can easily get quite lost along the way, without even realizing it, until it is sometimes too late. Scripture recounts the stories of many people who got lost along the way; some recovered, and some died lost, blind, and alone in their wildernesses.

Blind to Being Alone
In the book of Deuteronomy, there is a terrifying passage concerning the Israelites who were entering the Promised Land after wandering in the wilderness for forty years. The Israelites continually complained and doubted God, despite the fact that He performed miracle after miracle as He moved them from Egypt to the Promised Land. Moses was not even allowed into the Land that God promised to His people because the Lord was angry at Moses' disobedience. Moses wrote, "Even with me the Lord was angry on your account, saying, 'You shall not enter there'" (Deuteronomy 1:37). When hardships arose in the wilderness, the Israelites (the people Moses was leading into the Promised Land) continued to complain as they feared and doubted God; they wanted to return to slavery in Egypt and to the life they knew.

Finally, the Israelites admitted to Moses,

> "'We have sinned against the Lord! We are ready to go up and fight, just as the Lord our God commanded us'... But the Lord said to Moses, 'Say to them, Do not go up and fight, *for I am not in the midst of you;* otherwise you will be defeated by your enemies.' Although I told you, you would not listen. You rebelled against the command of the Lord and presumptuously went up into the hill country. The Amorites who lived in that hill country chased you as bees do. They beat you down in Seir as far as Hormah. When you returned and wept before the Lord, the Lord would neither heed your voice nor pay you any attention," (Deuteronomy 1:41a, 42-45; italics mine).

What a daunting passage, especially considering the fact that, like many of us, the Israelites did not know they were lost and on their own! They were totally blind to being lost.

Throughout the journey into the wilderness towards the Promised Land, like our own journeys through life, God promised to be with His people. However, when His people refused to listen, when they were obstinately disobedient, and when they decided when and where to go without consulting God, He said to the Israelites, "I am not in the midst of you"; I personally find this phrase more than alarming, and I do not want to go someplace where God is not with me! If we are apathetic or disobedient, then we can bring ourselves to a place where our hearts become so hardened that we can no longer even find God, and we will never recover ourselves. Scripture says, "Seek the Lord while he may be found, call upon him while he is near; let the wicked forsake their way, and the unrighteous their thoughts; let them turn to the Lord, that he may have mercy on them, and to our God, for he will abundantly pardon" (Isaiah 55:6-7). Most of us casually read Isaiah 55 and miss something quite important: the words,

"While he may be found." The words imply, logically, that there will be a time when God will no longer be found and when He is no longer in our midst! When we refuse to read God's Word, when we refuse to obey, when we continually go our own way, when we become complacent and lukewarm, then our hearts can become hardened and God may no longer be found. What a horrid place to be!

God spoke directly to Moses, who then relayed what God said to the Israelites. Today, God does not speak to us directly like He did with Moses, but He does still speak, most often through His Word, the Bible. I have heard many people say they do not hear God's voice, so they live in confusion, they go places where God never intended for them to go, and then they wonder what went wrong and how they got so lost. When people do not consistently read their Bible, preferably on a daily basis, then they wander in confusion, yet are unaware that they are quite lost. How many roads will a man walk until he admits he is lost? Apparently many!

Stumbling in the Dark
Many of us are merely ignorant of what path to take and repeatedly walk down all types of paths in our vain attempts to find the correct one. Some people fill their lives with the desire to entertain themselves through various diversions such as movies, television, books, or hobbies to fill the time and to bring some pleasure into life. Some people work incessantly in an attempt to live the American Dream in order to see how many material possessions they can accumulate, or how much money they can save in the bank. Some people think that everything is so senseless and futile that the pain, boredom, or monotony of life becomes overbearing for them; consequently, they turn to drugs or excessive alcohol consumption in order to numb these feelings. Some of us continue to walk down road after road, sometimes never discovering or admitting that we are truly lost. It never occurs

to many people that time could be spent in the study of God's Word by reading, going to Bible-study classes, seeking out spiritual mentors, or whatever it takes to understand how to live through Scripture. Unfortunately, it is often in the reality of dying that we finally understand life, ourselves, and the road we need to walk for the journey. It is most unfortunate when, after stumbling blindly through the majority of their lives, some people discover the road they were intended to walk while staring death in the face, so that the final chapter of their lives closes with regret.

Paul's Blindness
Paul became, arguably, the greatest Christian who ever lived. However, before he was a Christian, Paul literally became blind for three days when he thought he was serving God by hunting Christians down to imprison and even to kill them for following "The Way," which was a seemingly strange new religion known today as Christianity.

> "Meanwhile Saul [Paul] still breathing threats and murder against the disciples of the Lord, went to the high priest and asked him for letters to the synagogues at Damascus, so that if he found any who belonged to the Way, men or women, he might bring them bound to Jerusalem. Now as he was going along and approaching Damascus, suddenly a light from heaven flashed around him. He fell to the ground and heard a voice saying to him, 'Saul, Saul, why do you persecute me?' He asked, 'Who are you, Lord?' The reply came, 'I am Jesus, whom you are persecuting. But get up and enter the city, and you will be told what to do.' The men who were traveling with him stood speechless because they heard the voice but saw no one. Saul got up from the ground, and though his eyes were open, he could see nothing; so they led him by the hand and brought him to Damascus."
> (Acts 9:1-8)

Later, when God revealed Himself to Saul [Paul] again, his eyesight was restored; "So Ananias went and entered the house. He laid his hands on Saul and said, 'Brother Saul, the Lord Jesus, who appeared to you on your way here, has sent me that you may regain your sight and be filled with the Holy Spirit.' And immediately something like scales fell from his eyes, and his sight was restored" (Acts 9:17-18). Only God can restore our sight and rescue us from our blindness. We cannot see on our own. Paul was an extremely well-educated man, full of the knowledge of the Scriptures, and he belonged to the strictest sect of the Jewish religion (Acts 26:5); yet, he lived in blindness, which he was unaware of until Jesus showed him just how blind he was on that Damascus road. Jesus often shows us our blindness as well, though we sometimes refuse to listen. If we would read the Bible, we would know just how blind we truly are; however, if we do not read, we will lose ourselves.

Waiting for Old Age
One of the most foolish ideas that many people have is realizing the need to follow Christ, but putting it off. It seems as if many want to wait until they are old to do things the right way because there are sins or destructive lifestyles (though, at the time, unbeknownst to them) they want to live out **now.** How often do people somehow think there is more satisfaction in the "fleeting pleasures of sin" (Hebrews 11:24) than in the greater and lasting pleasures of walking with Jesus! These people say they will follow Christ when they are old, as if they are guaranteed to get old! Not all of us reach old age. Not all of us become hospice patients with chaplain visits and time to reflect, repent, pray, and contemplate life and death. Accidents happen. Murders occur. Heart attacks strike. The Bible also talks about this foolish type of thinking:

> "Be dressed and ready for action and have your lamps lit; be like those who are waiting for their master to return

from the wedding banquet, so that they may open the door for him as soon as he knocks. Blessed are those slaves whom the master finds alert when he comes; truly I tell you, he will fasten his belt and have them sit down to eat, and he will come and serve them. If he comes during the middle of the night, or near dawn, and finds them so, blessed are those slaves. But know this: if the owner of the house had known at what hour the thief was coming, he would not have let his house be broken into. You also must be ready, for the Son of Man is coming at an unexpected hour... Who then is the faithful and prudent manager whom his master will put in charge of his slaves, to give them their allowance of food at the proper time? Blessed is that slave whom his master finds at work when he arrives. Truly I tell you, he will put that one in charge of all his possessions. But if the slave says to himself, 'My master is delayed in coming' and if he begins to beat the other slaves, men and women, and to eat and drink and get drunk, the master of the slave will come on a day he does not expect him and at an hour that he does not know, and will cut him to pieces, and put him with the unfaithful. That slave who knew what his master wanted, but did not prepare himself or do what was wanted, will receive a severe beating."
(Luke 12:35-39 & 42-48)

How misguided it is to wait until old age to follow God. Jesus told many parables such as this one, which are recorded in Scripture, because He loves us and wants to reward us. Jesus does not want to punish us, but if we choose through our own free will to disobey and live far away from Him, He will allow us to do that, yet He warns us of the severe consequences. The Bible was given to us by a God who is so in love with us that He desires to speak to us on a daily basis and to be intimately involved in every area of our lives. He wants us to learn, to discover, and to live abundant, meaningful lives. There are numerous examples in Scripture that we can learn from, but if we do not read, then we fail to learn. Unfortunately, instead of learning through the mistakes of others, many often learn only by their own mistakes, when all they needed to do was to read His Blueprint for life and to follow His Plan. We could have saved ourselves great pains and foolish mistakes; I know, as I have often learned the hard way.

There were many great people in the Bible who made grave errors from which we can learn. One such man was King Solomon. Fortunately, Solomon was granted old age to contemplate his life, but how foolish it is for us to gamble on the opportunity Solomon was given, and to miss out on the abundant life here on earth and the heavenly rewards that await God's faithful servants.

Ecclesiastes
The Old Testament Wisdom book of Ecclesiastes records the recovery process of an old man, probably Solomon, the wisest man who has ever lived; but he found that, "All is vanity, and a chasing after the wind" (Ecclesiastes 1:14). Though some scholars debate this book's authorship, many believe King Solomon wrote this book since it begins with, "The words of the Teacher, the son of David, king of Jerusalem." For the purposes of this book, we will not debate authorship, but will assume King Solomon as the writer of Ecclesiastes.

The Hebrew name of the book of Ecclesiastes, and of the author, is "Qoheleth"; it comes from the root, "to assemble; to gather; to call together." This poetic book of Scripture is a gathering of wisdom through the loss and recovery of a man in his later years of life. Despite being so wise, Solomon was indeed quite lost throughout part of his life. Solomon walked down many, many roads until he finally admitted he had gotten lost along the way when he wrote the book of Ecclesiastes. How did Solomon lose himself? — In the same manner that we all lose ourselves: through a lost spirituality, a blind, directionless path toward the God of our own creation, and a human arrogance that ultimately becomes a path to destruction.

I have a friend who used to ask me, "Are we moving in the right direction?" If we are moving within Scripture, then yes, but if not, then no my friend, we are moving in the wrong direction. Solomon began to move in the wrong direction when he was led astray by his numerous wives, many whom he married outside of God's parameters. He took foreign wives who led him down spiritual paths of destruction. He allowed them to worship other gods, to sacrifice to those gods, and this lead Solomon away from Jehovah, the one true God whom his father King David worshipped and taught Solomon to love and worship. Solomon did not always heed his father's advice or the command of God, "You shall have no other gods before Me" (Exodus 20:3).

As one begins to move away from Scripture, the loss of the self begins.

No Other gods Before Me
What exactly does "You shall have no other gods before Me" mean? Many of us think about the story in Exodus 32 when the Israelites, including Aaron, thought that Moses had died since he was gone for so long on the mountain (40 days), and then made a golden calf, foolishly thinking they were worshipping the Lord with it; Aaron "took the gold from them, formed it in a mold, and cast an image of a calf; and they said, 'These are your gods, O Israel, who brought you out of the land of Egypt!' When Aaron saw this, he built an altar before it; and Aaron made proclamation and said, 'Tomorrow shall be a festival to the Lord" (Exodus 32:4-5).

We do not generally make golden calves or images that we

worship, mistakenly thinking we are worshipping God as Aaron did, but we often worship other "gods," such as materialism, our careers, people we place before God's commands, or anything that holds our affections above God, all of which can indeed be "other gods." However, I propose another god which all of us at times worship above Jesus Christ, our God, Lord, and Savior — the god of ourselves. Any time we are not totally and completely submitted to the lordship of Christ, and whenever we do what we feel is best (regardless of Scripture), we have placed a god before Him in ourselves. Have you ever known that you should avoid some action since it was contrary to Scripture, but went ahead and did it anyway? You were placing a god before Him — you and your own desires. Have you ever known that you were supposed to do something, but did not perform that function? You were placing a god before Him — you and your own desires. How often do we place a god before the one true God? — Often, and without even realizing it.

Solomon, like the rest of us, placed other gods before the one true God, which we can read about in Ecclesiastes. In addition to placing himself before God through his own desires, perhaps Solomon in his later years also placed his wealth, his pleasures, and his wisdom before God; perhaps he made these gifts "gods" instead of gifts given by God for His purposes.

Wealth
In Ecclesiastes, Solomon spoke of his great wealth. What do many of us spend our lives doing? — Acquiring wealth. For some, we work to provide for our selves or our families. Work is a necessary and good part of life, and even the apostle Paul said, "Anyone unwilling to work should not eat" (2 Thessalonians 3:10). For others though, work is not only a means to provide a home and food for themselves or their families, but it becomes an obsession, a god, and an attempt to get rich and acquire material luxuries that they convince

themselves that they need. Solomon wrote, "I made great works; I built houses and planted vineyards for myself; I made myself gardens and parks, and planted in them all kinds of fruit trees. I made pools from which to water the forest of growing trees. I bought male and female slaves, and had slaves who were born in my house; I also had great possessions of herds and flocks, more than any who had been before me in Jerusalem. I also gathered for myself silver and gold and the treasure of kings and of the provinces."
(Ecclesiastes 2:4-8a).

What was the purpose of all this wealth? For Solomon, it was all vanity, as he concluded that, "I hated my toil in which I had toiled under the sun, seeing that I must leave it to those who come after me — and who knows whether they will be wise or foolish? Yet they will be master of all for which I toiled and used my wisdom under the sun. This also is vanity. So I turned and gave my heart up to despair concerning all the toil of my labors under the sun, because sometimes one who has toiled with wisdom and knowledge and skill must leave all to be enjoyed by another who did not toil for it. This also is vanity and a great evil. What do mortals get from all the toil and strain with which they toil under the sun? For all their days are full of pain, and their work is a vexation; even at night their minds do not rest. This also is vanity" (Ecclesiastes 2:18-23). Solomon also concluded, when pondering wealth, "The lover of money will not be satisfied with money; nor the lover of wealth with gain. This is also vanity" (Ecclesiastes 5:10). Many of us begin to lose ourselves in this struggle for material possessions, even though Scripture warns, "For the love of money is the root of all kinds of evil, and in their eagerness to be rich, some have wandered away from the faith and pierced themselves with many pains" (I Timothy 6:10).

Scripture and Wealth
As Christians, we should never be at home in this world or feel

comfortable within society. The media (in all its forms) and society (in general) bombards us with the "need" to acquire wealth. We "need" larger homes, newer cars, nicer furniture, and every household gadget available to make our lives easier and more "productive." Advertising is a huge market, enticing us into a vicious cycle of debt. Hebrews 13:5 says, "Keep your lives free from the love of money, and be content with what you have." How many of us are truly content with what we have? Paul wrote, "I have learned to be content with whatever I have. I know what it is to have little, and I know what it is to have plenty. In any and all circumstances I have learned the secret of being well-fed and of going hungry, of having plenty and of being in need. I can do all things through him who strengthens me" (Philippians 4:11-13). Notice Paul wrote that he had *learned* to be content; it is not natural to be so, but is a learned attitude. All of us who can read these words can learn to live in contentment.

Jesus knew the greed in our hearts when He said, "Do not store up for yourselves treasures on earth, where moth and rust consume and where thieves break in and steal; but store up for yourselves treasures in heaven, where neither moth nor rust consumes and where thieves do not break in and steal. For where your treasure is, there your heart will be also" (Matthew 6:19-21). Jesus continued in His teaching and said, "No one can serve two masters; for a slave will either hate the one and love the other, or be devoted to the one and despise the other. You cannot serve God and wealth" (Matthew 6:24).

There is a story about the difficulty of wealth in the Gospel of Mark:
> "As he [Jesus] was setting out on a journey, a man ran up and knelt before him, and asked him, 'Good Teacher, what must I do to inherit eternal life?'..." Jesus answered him and said, "You know the commandments: 'You shall

not murder; You shall not commit adultery; You shall not bear false witness; You shall not defraud; Honor your father and mother.' He said to him, 'Teacher, I have kept all these since my youth.' Jesus, looking at him, loved him and said, 'You lack one thing; go, sell what you own, and give the money to the poor, and you will have treasure in heaven; then come, follow me.' When he heard this, he was shocked and went away grieving, for he had many possessions. Then Jesus looked around and said to his disciples, 'How hard it will be for those who have wealth to enter the kingdom of God!' And the disciples were perplexed at these words. But Jesus said to them again, 'Children, how hard it is to enter the kingdom of God! It is easier for a camel to go through the eye of a needle than for someone rich to enter the kingdom of God'" (Mark 10:17-25).

Please do not misunderstand the point Jesus was making. He did not say money, in and of itself, is evil; otherwise, God would not have given Solomon so much wealth. There is no intrinsic evil to wealth. Jesus was teaching about the human heart. He was teaching about motives and what many of us do for or with wealth. There are many wonderful, wealthy Christians who bless others with their money, but it is often in our attitudes where we sin and get lost, such as the attitude of greed or covetousness.

With a little wandering away from Scripture, one begins to get lost.

Pleasure
Solomon also desired to live for pleasure, as he wrote,

> "I searched with my mind how to cheer my body with wine… and how to lay hold of folly, until I might see what was good for mortals to do under heaven during the few days of their life… I got singers, both men and women,

and delights of the flesh, and many concubines" (Ecclesiastes 2:3&8). He went on to say, "Whatever my eyes desired I did not keep from them; I kept my heart from no pleasure in all my toil, and this was my reward for my toil. Then I considered all that my hands had done and the toil I had spent doing it, and again, all was vanity and a chasing after the wind, and there was nothing to be gained under the sun" (Ecclesiastes 2:10-11).

We can also lose ourselves in sensuality. Our normal, human desires can become addictive and sinful desires of the flesh when we move away from Scripture. When Solomon spoke of pleasure, he mentioned two areas of pleasure that he indulged himself in: wine and women. Wine, in and of itself, is not sinful. In His very first miracle, Jesus made wine for His friends at the wedding in Cana (John 2:1-11) as He was possibly declaring Himself here as the True Vine (John 15:1) at the start of His ministry. Psalm 104:15 says wine, "gladdens the human heart," but Scripture also warns of avoiding drunkenness and addiction to wine, both of which are sin (Galatians 5:21, Ephesians 5:18, Titus 1:7).

By reading Scripture, we can hopefully understand the correct and incorrect use of wine/alcohol in the life of a Christian. However, the reader must also keep in mind that if drinking wine causes another to stumble, then its consumption should be avoided. Paul wrote, "But take care that this liberty of yours does not somehow become a stumbling block" (1 Corinthians 8:9). Paul was referring to a pagan practice in his day of sacrificing food to idols, and whether or not Christians should eat such food. American culture does not understand such practices as sacrificing food to idols. However, within the concept of our freedom in Christ and living as a witness of the love of Jesus to others, this same principle Paul spoke about concerning food can be applied to drinking wine. We cannot allow our liberty to be a stumbling block for others. Whenever we are unsure of how to live, once again, the answers can be found in the Bible, but it must be read to gain that knowledge! We cannot simply live by doing whatever seems right in our own eyes. We must always consult Scripture, and we must always put others before ourselves.

Solomon also wrote of the many women he loved in his life, and the pleasure he sought in his sexuality. Sex is a beautiful, spiritual gift from God, to be enjoyed between a man and his wife in the full expression of love and commitment towards one another by the joining of two people that they may become one flesh (Genesis 2:24). There is an entire book of the Bible (Song of Solomon) devoted to the beauty of human love and sexuality, as God intends. Yet, Scripture warns more times than I can count about the dangers of sexual immorality and how fornication, adultery, and homosexuality are sins not only against God, but against one's own body, which is the temple of the Holy Spirit (1 Corinthians 3:16, & 6:9-20). Pleasure and sensuality so easily become gods. Our normal, human passions can lead us away from obedience to God and the boundaries that are placed in the Bible for our own safety when we seek to enjoy them apart from God's design as recorded in Scripture.

God created sex for procreation and for our pleasure, though He placed protective boundaries around it for our physical, emotional and spiritual health. "So God created humankind in his image, in the image of God he created them; male and female he created them. So God blessed them, and God said to them, 'Be fruitful and multiply, and fill the earth and subdue it" (Genesis 1:27-28). One of the first "commands" God gave to humankind was to have sex, but God set up protections for us within these commands so that it would go well with us because He loves us so deeply and because He wants us to experience the full and complete pleasure of our sexuality. One such protection is that sex must only be enjoyed within the sacrificial covenant of marriage:

"Let marriage be held in honor by all, and let the marriage bed be kept undefiled; for God will judge fornicators and adulterers" (Hebrews 13:4). What is a fornicator? — It is an unmarried person who has sex outside of the covenant of marriage. What is an adulterer? — It is a person who has sex with a married person who is not their spouse, but the spouse of another. Why does God have such a "narrow" view of sex? — Because sex is the union, both bodily and spiritually, of a man and his wife, who love one another, sacrifice for one another, are fully committed to one another, and who are willing to lay down their lives for one another as Christ laid down His life for us. Marriage represents the most intimate relationship between Christ and us, the Church, His Bride. The apostle Paul wrote about marriage as it represents a Christian's relationship to Christ in his letter to the Ephesians:

> "Husbands, love your wives, just as Christ loved the church and gave himself up for her, in order to make her holy by cleansing her with the washing of water by the word, so as to present the church to himself in splendor, without a spot or wrinkle or anything of any kind — yes, so that she may be holy and without blemish. In the same way, husbands should love their wives as they do their own bodies. He who loves his wife loves himself. For no one ever hates his own body, but he nourishes and tenderly cares for it, just as Christ does for the church, because we are members of his body. 'For this reason a man will leave his father and mother and be joined to his wife, and the two will become one flesh.' This is a great mystery, and I am applying it to Christ and the church" (Ephesians 5:25-32).

Sex is the physical, human representation of the love and intimacy between Christ and His Bride, the Church. God made a covenant with us, His Bride, as husbands and wives make a covenant with one another. The marriage covenant is consummated with sex, the joining of two people into one… two lives into one life. Breaking the marriage/sexual covenant with another person therefore represents breaking covenant with God. God takes this covenantal relationship quite seriously, which is why sex is so important to God and is to be enjoyed only within the marriage relationship.

We are also made in the image of God. In the possible creation of another life that only comes through sex, we share in one image of God by participating in creation — life itself, through the pleasure and beauty of sex. As a single mom, who got pregnant more than thirty years ago and had my son out of wedlock, I feel at liberty to stress this point: children should be born to a mother and father, a family unit, in the security and bond of marriage. Raising a child alone is very difficult. Granted, some spouses die or leave the home, and there are no guarantees of the family unit, but having a child as a single parent brings certain difficulties and hardships. There are usually financial hardships. There are hardships of time and care for the child. Most importantly, the child misses out on the male figure head and the fatherly discipline and love that differs from a mother's. In a single-parent home, there is the lack of a role model of either a woman/mother or a man/father, depending on which parent is absent in raising the child, and the child is the one who suffers. Both influences, a mother and a father, are God's design for child-rearing because they provide the intended atmosphere for a healthy, balanced child.

Adultery is a very painful sin. If a man, for instance, wanders and cheats on his wife, he has hurt her, sometimes beyond repair, since he has broken trust (which may never be regained), broken their intimate union, and shared his intimacy with another. He became one flesh with another person, and consequently shattered that deep, trusting, intimate relationship of a husband and wife. A spouse cannot be one unit, in body and soul, with two people. Scripture warns in numerous places of the sin and foolishness of adultery, especially in the book of Proverbs.

Many of us have had sexual relationships outside of marriage. When that relationship ends, the pain is greater if sex was involved than if the two people were not sexually active. Why? — Because sex is a joining of both the body and the soul. Sex creates a oneness between two people, and when one partner leaves, a portion of the soul is ripped apart. It is neither natural nor healthy to move in and out of sexual relationships and it is foolish not to understand the damage that is inflicted with a break-up. God is NOT against sex! He created it, and He created it for procreation and for pleasure. He does not want us hurt and He does not want people to be used as objects for pleasure. Life, especially human life, is valued highly by God, and His boundaries display his deep love. God commands us to love one another and to view others not as means to an end (such as mere gratification), but to understand people as ends in themselves, to be respected, loved, enjoyed completely in all respects, not just sexually, and to be valued above all of creation.

The risk of sexually-transmitted diseases is also a very real and serious threat that does not occur within a loving, monogamous, marital relationship. Diseases are not necessarily a punishment from God; they are merely the natural result of behaviors that were never intended. God continues to try to protect humanity, yet humanity continues to spurn His loving guidelines of safety.

Scripture and Pleasure
God desires His children to experience pleasure. God took pleasure in creating, and He continues to take pleasure in His

creation. God gave humanity a pleasurable means of creating life as well with sex. God takes pleasure in blessing us: "Blessed be the God and Father of our Lord Jesus Christ, who has blessed us with every spiritual blessing in the heavenly places, just as he chose us in Christ before the foundation of the world to be holy and blameless before him in love. He destined us for adoption as his children through Jesus Christ, according to the good pleasure of his will, to the praise of his glorious grace that he freely bestowed on us in the Beloved" (Ephesians 1:3-6). Jesus experienced fun and pleasure when He lived on earth. He went to weddings and parties, He laughed with his disciples, He ate good meals and enjoyed wine, He told stories and He enjoyed people. There is nothing sinful about pleasure, but pleasure, like all things in life, has its boundaries and its rightful place.

Our attitudes and motivations are also taken into consideration by God. For example, "By faith, Moses, when he was grown up, refused to be called a son of Pharaoh's daughter, choosing rather to share ill-treatment with the people of God than to enjoy the fleeting pleasures of sin" (Hebrews 11:24-25). Moses could have remained comfortable in the home of Pharaoh when he lived in the luxury of his Egyptian household, but instead, he chose obedience to God over the "fleeting pleasures of sin." God created pleasurable things for us in life, but within His boundaries, for our own well-being.

With a little wandering away from Scripture, one begins to get lost.

Wisdom
Solomon continued his contemplations in Ecclesiastes and wrote of another "god" that, on the surface, appears to be quite noble — wisdom. He wrote,

"So I turned to consider wisdom and madness and folly;

for what can the one do who comes after the king? Only what has been done. Then I saw that wisdom excels folly as light excels darkness. The wise have eyes in their head, but fools walk in darkness. Yet I perceived the same fate befalls all of them. Then I said to myself, 'What happens to the fool will happen to me also; why then have I been so very wise?' And I said to myself that this also is vanity. For there is no enduring remembrance of the wise or of fools, seeing that in the days to come all will have been long forgotten. How can the wise die just like fools? ...for all is vanity and a chasing after the wind" (Ecclesiastes 2:12-17).

Some of us take pride in our educations and our degrees, and some of us rely on our own knowledge for the answers we need, forgetting that Scripture says, "There is a way that seems right to a man, but in the end leads only to death" (Proverbs 16:25). Also, "Trust in the Lord with all your heart, and do not rely on your own understanding. In all your ways acknowledge Him, and He will make straight your paths" (Proverbs 3:5-6). Our educations and our self-perceived wisdom is nothing but folly or foolishness to God; "Do not deceive yourselves. If you think that you are wise in this age, you should become fools so that you may become wise. For the wisdom of this world is foolishness with God. For it is written, 'He catches the wise in their craftiness' and again, 'The Lord knows the thoughts of the wise, that they are futile' (I Corinthians 3:18-20). Our own knowledge and educations can make us blind to true wisdom.

Scripture and Wisdom
"For the wisdom of this world is foolishness with God" (1 Corinthians 3:19). God *wants* to give us wisdom. The book of James says, "If any of you is lacking in wisdom, ask God, who gives to all generously and ungrudgingly, and it will be given to you" (James 1:5). However, there is a foolish, worldly wisdom

which profits nothing, though many of us pride ourselves in it, and there is wisdom from God, which is found in Scripture. Again, our motivation for wisdom, like anything else, is important to God. Why did God grant so much wisdom to Solomon? I Kings conveys the story of how Solomon obtained his wisdom:

> "At Gibeon the Lord appeared to Solomon in a dream by night; and God said, 'Ask what I should give you.' And Solomon said, 'You have shown great and steadfast love to your servant my father David, because he walked before you in faithfulness, in righteousness, and in uprightness of heart toward you: and you have kept for him this great and steadfast love, and have given him a son to sit on his throne today. And now, O Lord my God, you have made your servant king in place of my father David, although I am only a little child: I do not know how to go out or come in. And your servant is in the midst of the people whom you have chosen, a great people so numerous they cannot be numbered or counted. Give your servant therefore an understanding mind to govern your people, able to discern between good and evil: for who can govern this great people?' It pleased the Lord that Solomon had asked this. God said to him, 'Because you have asked this, and have not asked for yourself long life or riches, or for the life of your enemies, but have asked for yourself understanding to discern what is right, I now do according to your word. Indeed I give you a wise and discerning mind; no one like you has been before you and no one like you shall arise after you'" (1 Kings 3:5-12).

God gave Solomon such great wisdom because in humility, Solomon knew his limitations to govern and to be king, and he desired to be a great leader like his father David. In other words, Solomon asked for something with which he could benefit others. Unfortunately, Solomon was distracted and was led away from following God when he married outside of God's parameters and allowed his foreign wives to worship other gods, which he also foolishly followed.

> "For when Solomon was old, his wives turned away his heart after other gods; and his heart was not true to the Lord his God, as was the heart of his father David... So Solomon did what was evil in the sight of the Lord, and did not completely follow the Lord, as his father David had done" (1 Kings 11:4 & 6).

Scripture describes the down-fall of Solomon, which began when he wandered away from the wisdom God gave him. Solomon allowed deceptions to creep into his mind and heart. "Then the Lord was angry with Solomon, because his heart turned away from the Lord, the God of Israel, who had appeared to him twice, and had commanded him concerning this matter, that he should not follow other gods; but he did not observe what the Lord commanded. Therefore the Lord said to Solomon, 'Since this has been your mind and you have not kept my covenant and my statutes that I have commanded you, I will surely tear the kingdom from you and give it to your servant. Yet for the sake of your father David I will not do it in your lifetime; I will tear it out of the hand of your son'" (1 Kings 11:9-12). God then raised up many adversaries against Solomon, which plagued him for the rest of his life. Perhaps it was during this time that Solomon, in his regretful reflections, wrote Ecclesiastes.

With a little wandering away from Scripture, one begins to get lost.

"For the time is coming when people will not put up with sound doctrine, but having itching ears, they will accumulate for themselves teachers to suit their own desires, and will turn away from listening to the truth and wander away into myths."

(2 Timothy 4:3-4)

CHAPTER TWO

The Deceptions in Life

God on Our Terms
Most of us, perhaps all of us in varying degrees, want God on our own terms. We want God to be who we want Him to be. We want to create our own God, and we do this quite often without even realizing it. We want God to go along with our plans and desires. We want God, in a sense, to give in to us, rather than us giving up our very lives to Him by being totally surrendered to His Word as He demands. We live in such deception, thinking God will merely go along with us, and that He will actually become whomever we want Him to be. Many of us are so deceived. The only way out of our deceptions is through looking at exactly what God's Word says.

The Old Testament Laws, especially those found in the books of Exodus and Leviticus, are very, very specific in explaining exactly how God's people were to sacrifice, how they were to construct the Tabernacle for worship, and how they were to perform many tasks in both religious and daily life. The minutia of these Old Testament laws can become laborious to read, but the point is that we come to God on **His** terms, and never on **our** terms. We cannot approach God however and whenever we desire and yet be correct, for we must consult the Bible, and we must approach Him as He commands. We cannot live in Scriptural ignorance, making it up as we go along, and yet think we are Christians. Scripture, and not our own minds, instructs us in how to live in relational love to God and to others. Many "Christians" do not love God by living in complete surrender to Him, which is what Scripture commands, nor do they live in sacrificial love towards others, which is also a command and not an option! Any time we live for what makes **us** happy, instead of through the lens of what is pleasing to God and for the good of others, we are not living as Christians. Yet, how can we possibly begin to know how to live in the manner that God commands if we do not know what God's Word says? We can be so easily deceived.

Satan is the master of deception, and the Bible refers to him as the "Father of lies" (John 8:44). In the book of Job, the story begins by saying, "One day the heavenly beings came to present themselves before the Lord, and Satan also came among them. The Lord said to Satan, 'Where have you come from?' Satan answered, 'From going to and fro on the earth, and from walking up and down on it.'" (Job 1:6-7). Today, Satan continues to investigate the earth: "Like a roaring lion your adversary the devil prowls around, looking for someone to devour" (1 Peter 5:8). Satan is busy deceiving and devouring many people, often in places where God is sought; but, because of Scriptural ignorance, God is not discovered.

Deceptions in Desperation
There is a saying, "Desperate people do desperate things." Desperate people are also desperate for answers, which is where the "roaring lion" deceives and devours. One such place is in Alcoholics Anonymous. AA is a wonderful Twelve Step program that has helped countless alcoholics turn their lives around and become sober, productive, happy people; I have nothing but praise for this group. However, Satan is alive and well in AA, just as he is all over the world; yet, he has a

captive, desperate audience in AA who provide him with an easy target: themselves.

Step Three of the Twelve Steps says that we, "Made a decision to turn our will and our lives over to the care of God <u>as we understood Him</u>" (Twelve Steps, 34). This is a wonderful step, especially for those people who have a "problem" with God, who want nothing to do with Him, who grew up in the Church and were disgusted, hurt, or angry with God because of some situation that perhaps occurred within the Church. However, there is a danger in the third step, as God can therefore be pretty much anything we want Him to be in our finite, sinful understanding.

When I conducted spirituality groups in an AA/NA recovery program as a chaplain, one woman told me her god, as she "understood him," was a rock. God is then, in this step, limited to who we fantasize Him to be, though our understanding may be nowhere near who God actually is. According to Step Three, each of us can therefore, in our own unique imaginations, create "God." We become the creator, rather than acknowledging God as Creator. In doing so, we become our own god and we make God, the true Creator, a Being we create in our own minds. How dangerous! However, God did reveal Himself to us in the Bible, through Jesus Christ; so, while we will never understand God completely, we can know Him personally, and at least have an understanding of who He is. God is not a mere, inanimate rock.

Step Three is at least a start, but it is only a start. Unfortunately, many alcoholics/addicts who have now found their own god, as they "understood him," believe this understanding makes them a Christian. Understanding God in our own imaginations never goes further than our concept of who we want God to be, and the god of our creation and imagination becomes the god of our own delusion. AA's manual, though it is well-intentioned, often replaces (rather than accompanies) the Bible for "Christians," and IS the recovered alcoholics' Bible. Without knowing God through Scripture, AA's manual (The Big Book) can leave the recovered addict with an imaginary god and a blueprint for life based only on a limited human imagination. The recovered alcoholic lives by the Big Book's rules for sobriety rather than through the living and True God of the Bible. Satan is most pleased.

I have a friend who has been sober for about fifteen years through AA. He attends meetings twice per week (religiously), though he does not always attend church, and he does not attend any type of Bible study. He can cite chapter and page of the Big Book, but he knows little about the Bible. He believes that, because he talks about God and says the Serenity Prayer, he is a Christian; however, he has a limited understanding about the Christian faith and the Bible. He knows a little **about** God, but Christians know God personally through a life-changing experience in Jesus Christ, and they live as Christ-followers through the power of the Holy Spirit. My now sober friend informed me that, when he got to Step Three, he heard a friend say, "If your god doesn't work for you, fire him and get a new one!" (This comment is not the opinion of AA). Basically, you do whatever you need to do to stay sober, including creating the Creator to fit your whims. I did not think this comment was very sound advice, though perhaps I misunderstood the intent. I pray that what my friend meant to say was that a new or different understanding of God is what was needed in order to become sober. Perhaps many of us have an incorrect understanding and view of God, which therefore prevents our recoveries. However, if we read the Bible, we can get a correct view of God and avoid many of life's pitfalls.

The god of one's own making and imagination is like the golden calf that Aaron made for the Israelites when Moses was gone for so long on the mountain. The Israelites constructed their own god made of gold, while Aaron actually believed they were worshipping Jehovah, the God Moses was with on the mountain. Aaron said about the golden calf, "These are your gods, O Israel, who brought you up out of the land of Egypt... Tomorrow shall be a festival to the Lord" (Exodus 32:4-5). Aaron was sadly mistaken, and God, in His anger, sent Moses back down to see this abomination; God punished the people for their foolish deception:

> "The Lord said to Moses, 'Go down at once! Your people, whom you brought up out of the land of Egypt, have acted perversely; they have been quick to turn aside from the way that I commanded them; they have cast for themselves an image of a calf, and have worshiped it and sacrificed to it, and said, 'These are your gods, O Israel, who brought you up out of the land of Egypt!' The Lord said to Moses, 'I have seen this people, how stiff-necked they are. Now let me alone, so that my wrath may burn hot against them and I may consume them" (Exodus 32:7-10).

God was ready to destroy the Israelites when they created their own god, though He relented and spared their lives. God is not whoever we want Him to be. He is God! When Moses asked God who He was, God said, "I AM WHO I AM" (Exodus 3:14). He is not whoever or whatever we create Him to be. He is the King of Kings and the Lord of Lords, the Creator of the Universe, who is more powerful than we could even begin to imagine. God is not some little item we can put in a box or mold into whatever it is we want Him to be that fits into our model that "works for us." We, the King's subjects, work for Him. How Satan deceives! It is truly terrifying!

Satan enters programs like AA, NA, and spirituality groups for people who are desperate for change and a form of spirituality. However, Satan blinds them into thinking they have actually found God, when what they have found is a demonic counterfeit; but that is who Satan is — he mimics the works of God in clever, deceptive ways, leading many astray to their destruction. Satan is hard at work in many places like AA, NA, and also in the Church, where people know they need to change, but instead of being changed by Jesus, they are sometimes deceived, changed, and influenced by the enemy, though they are totally unaware of that deception and distortion. The apostle Paul knew the slyness of Satan, and he urged others to remain close to Jesus and His Word so that they would not be led astray "That Satan might not outwit us, for we are not unaware of his schemes" (II Corinthians 2:10b). How could we ever be aware of the schemes of Satan unless we are aware of what Scripture has to say concerning his deceptions?

Parables

Jesus spoke in many parables about evil deceptions, one of which is recorded in Matthew 13:25-30. Jesus gave the following parable:

> "The kingdom of heaven may be compared to someone who sowed good seed in his field; but while everyone was asleep, an enemy came and sowed weeds among the wheat, and then went away. So when the plants came up and bore grain, then the weeds appeared as well. And the slaves of the householder came and said to him, 'Master, did you not sow good seed in your field? Where, then, did these weeds come from?' He answered, 'An enemy has done this.' The slaves said to him, 'Then do you want us to go and gather them?' But he replied, 'No; for in gathering the weeds you would uproot the wheat along with them. Let them both grow together until the harvest; and at the harvest time I will tell the reapers, Collect the weeds first and bind them in bundles to be burned, but gather the wheat into my barn.'"

Satan brings in deceptions, but God then brings people into meetings or churches, and into the lives of those being deceived in order to help and redirect them. Sadly, those who are deceived often do not listen. Anyone can be deceived. Scripture warns over and over, "Let no one deceive you with empty words, for because of these things the wrath of God comes on those who are disobedient" (Ephesians 5:6). How do we know if we are being deceived? — Our "fruits" will tell us. Are we living as Christ-followers, loving God, loving our neighbor as ourselves, denying our own selfish desires, taking up our crosses and following Jesus wherever He leads us? — or, are we hurting others? Are we living in some form of deception, lying to others, living a double life, cheating on anyone, living in addictions of any kind? Matthew 7:16 says, "You will know them by their fruits." 2 John 1:7 says, "Many deceivers have gone into the world." In Mark 13 we are warned that even the elect can be led astray with deceptions. How do we know if we are being deceived? We will know through Scripture, which tells us all truths, but again, if we do not know what is in the Bible, we will never know when we are being deceived. Some day, when we leave this earth and are face-to-face with God, we cannot say, "But I did not know!" Did you have a Bible? Did you simply fail to read it? Did you have a loving friend or pastor who tried to help you but you would not listen? Did you know, deep down, that you were deceived, but you enjoyed your sin too much? We will not have an excuse for living in deceptions since God Himself said through the prophets, "My people are destroyed for lack of knowledge" (Hosea 4:6). In our lack of knowledge is where we become deceived simply because we did not want to read the Bible.

The First Deception
Consider the very beginning of humanity and its relationship with God. In Genesis, the first book of the Bible, the problem of wanting God on our terms arose, and humankind was deceived. God gave the entire earth to His crowning creation,

man and woman; He gave them everything except one tree, the Tree of the Knowledge of Good and Evil (see chapter endnote). Genesis chapter two states,

> "The Lord God took the man and put him in the Garden of Eden to till it and keep it. And the Lord God commanded the man, 'You may freely eat of every tree of the garden; but of the Tree of the Knowledge of Good and Evil you shall not eat, for in the day that you eat of it you shall die'" (Genesis 2:15-17). God gave the rules, but they were not satisfactory to humans; they wanted their own rules, and the freedom to do whatever they wanted. Apparently, Adam and Eve did not believe God. They wanted God to bend to their desires, which is always a sure path to destruction. So what happened next? Satan came along with his deception, and God's words got slightly twisted: "Now the serpent was more crafty than any other wild animal that the Lord God had made. He said to the woman, 'Did God say, 'You shall not eat from any tree in the garden?' The woman said to the serpent, 'We may eat of the fruit of the trees of the garden, but God said, 'You shall not eat of the fruit of the tree that is in the middle of the garden, *nor shall you touch it*, or you shall die'" (Genesis 3:1-4 - italics mine).

First of all, Satan tried to confuse and deceive the woman when he questioned God's words. Satan asked the woman a question; in response to Satan's elusive words of deception, Eve responded with fragments of what God spoke, that they could indeed eat from the trees, but just not from the tree in the middle of the garden. Eve then added additional words that God never said; He never said, *"nor shall you touch it."* Right away, there was some confusion, which Satan always brings. Satan replied, "You will not die; for God knows that when you eat of it your eyes will be opened and you will be like God, knowing good and evil" (Genesis 3:4-5). Satan's statement was partially true, like all of his deceptions; they would indeed know good from evil. "So the woman saw that the tree was good for food, and that it was a delight to the eyes, and that the tree was to be desired to make one wise, she took of its fruit and ate" (Genesis 3:6). God's words regarding the forbidden tree were not delivered as a suggestion — they were a strict command. Could God not accept us doing something that *appeared* to be good, even though He said it was not? We would often like to have a god without protective boundaries, like teenagers would like to have parents without protective rules. We would like to have a god who makes us comfortable, who does not mind our sinful desires and who will give in to our weaknesses. We would want to "fire" any other god, since a holy, righteous, and just God might discipline us for our own good. God does not back down from His words because we perceive them differently, because we want to change their meaning, or because we simply do not agree. God never becomes the god we want him to be. He simply is who He is! He is "I AM WHO I AM."

I had an old pastor friend who used to say, "God said it, I believe it; that settles it!" We must take God and His Word on His terms — not ours. We all know the rest of the Eden story... disaster, which always strikes when we do not take God's Words seriously, when we try to have God on our terms rather than on His, and when we consequently live in deception. God clearly said, "You are free to eat from any tree in the garden; but you must not eat from the tree of the knowledge of good and evil, for when you eat of it you will surely die" (Genesis 2:16-17). God's words of course proved true, as we all do indeed die. God never lies. God's words always come to pass (Proverbs 30:5). God said He will not be mocked (Galatians 6:7). God's words always come to pass, though most of us do not believe God; if we did, we would not be so disobedient, we would live according to Scripture, and we would surely live our lives much differently than we do. We continually try to "persuade" God to bend to our ideas of who we think He is or who we want Him to be, and to become the god of our imaginations. Do we really think God will not notice our disobedience, or will change His mind, or perhaps even bend and give in to our distorted human logic and weaknesses? We often choose to live in deception, to remain blind and lost, and we deceive ourselves into thinking we know where we are going, while we stumble through unnecessary pain and confusion.

False Teachers

Scripture often warns of deceptions and people falling away from the Lord because they are deceived and are hearing only what they want to hear. 1 Timothy 4:1-2 says, "Now the Spirit expressly says that in latter times some will renounce the faith by paying attention to deceitful spirits and teachings of demons, through the hypocrisy of liars whose consciences are seared with a hot iron." Paul warned the church in Ephesus about deceptions when he wrote, "Let no one deceive you with empty words, for because of these things the wrath of God comes on those who are disobedient" (Ephesians 5:6). The wrath of God will come whether we believe in a God of wrath or not. If you believe only in a God of love, but not in a God who also demands holiness, you will be sorely disappointed, to put it mildly. There are two sides of God: love and holiness. Our understanding of him is incomplete if we focus only on His love and forget about His demand for holiness. The Bible clearly speaks of both sides of God: "Note then the kindness and the severity of God; severity towards those who have fallen, but God's kindness toward you, provided you continue in his kindness; otherwise you also will be cut off."
(Romans 11:22)

Jesus knew people could easily be deceived, and that there will always be those to deceive us. He said in Matthew 7:15-20:

> "Beware of false prophets, who come to you in sheep's clothing, but inwardly are ravenous wolves. You will know them by their fruits. Are grapes gathered from thorns, or figs from thistles? In the same way, every good tree bears good fruit, but the bad tree bears bad fruit. A good tree cannot bear bad fruit, nor can a bad tree bear good fruit. Every tree that does not bear good fruit is cut down and thrown into the fire. Thus you will know them by their fruits."

Through these words of Jesus, we can decipher truth from deception when we look at a person's "fruits" or his/her life. Peter also gives an example of these false teachers in 2 Peter 2:1-3:

> "But false prophets also arose among the people, just as there will be false teachers among you, who will secretly bring in destructive opinions. They will even deny the Master who brought them — bringing swift destruction on themselves. Even so, many will follow their licentious ways, and because of these teachers the way of truth will be maligned. And in their greed they will exploit you with deceptive words. Their condemnation, pronounced long ago, has not been idle, and their destruction is not asleep."

II Peter chapter 2 goes on to state what will happen to these false teachers, and how they lead others astray, hearing only what they want to hear, trying to squeeze God into their own molds, deceiving themselves and trying to serve God on their own terms. It simply does not ever work! Unfortunately, some people are unaware of the trap of deception and false teachings because they do not know what the Bible has to say about them. Why do many refuse to read? The Bible is a clear Blueprint for how to avoid the traps and deceptions we can so easily fall into.

With a little wandering away from Scripture, one gets lost.

> Note: For further insightful information regarding the Tree of the Knowledge of God and Evil, read the book *Did God Plant the Forbidden Tree?* and the book *The Knowledge of Good and Evil*, both by Joshua Collins, (GlobalEdAdvance Press).

"You must therefore be careful to do as the Lord your God has commanded you; you shall not turn to the right or to the left. You must follow exactly the path the Lord your God has commanded you so that you may live, and that it may go well with you."

(Deuteronomy 5:32-33)

CHAPTER THREE

Defining the Terms

Pilots, Crocodiles, and Cakes
I have a friend who said something very unusual to me one day. I asked my friend about his Christian faith and how much of the Bible he knows and reads, since we are commanded to live according to Scripture. He replied, "My Christianity is like a piece of music; when you don't have the sheet music in front of you, and you're not sure which exact notes to sing, you just listen, and you sing in the spirit of the music. You don't have to have it exact and perfect. I live in the spirit of my faith, and just do the best I can."

Here, before me, was a very intelligent, kind, considerate, "spiritual" man, yet he thought God left us without a Blueprint and that we would simply guess our way through life and do the best we could. Since my friend rarely reads his Bible, he is therefore left to do the best that he can because he refuses to read the map. My friend's way of life did not seem very clear to me, and his statement was rather difficult to understand in light of the Bible, so I asked him, "Are you a Christian?"

He replied, "Well, maybe not according to YOUR definition," as if we all have our own subjective definitions and versions of what a Christian is… it is like asking, for instance, to define a pilot. A pilot is a person who flies an airplane; I cannot give that specific definition while you may say a pilot is a person who hunts crocodiles or who bakes cakes. We cannot all have our own definition of what a pilot is. A pilot is a person who flies planes — that is what a pilot is. It is not one thing for you and another for me. The next time you get on an airplane and the pilot is sitting at the controls, would it be ok with you if he says that his definition of a pilot is not one who has been trained and licensed to fly planes but rather to hunt crocodiles? — and then he goes on to identify himself as a crocodile hunter or, in his definition, a "pilot?" His definition does not need to be the same as yours, right? He is just going to fly in the spirit of the wind and do the best he can. Let's see how quickly you put on your seat belt and wait for take off!

So what is a Christian? It is not one thing for you and another for me. A Christian is objectively defined as one who is a Christ-follower, which is how we arrived at that name. How do we follow Christ? We follow our Savior by His example, by obeying His commands, and by loving God and our neighbor as ourselves, which sums up the whole Law (Leviticus 19:18, quoted in Mathew 19:19). How on earth can we possibly know what Jesus did or taught unless we read about His life and His teachings, which are found in Scripture? How can we possibly claim to be a Christian if we do not read the Bible or know what is in it? How can we follow Christ if we do not know what He did, what He taught, and who He is? Without a firm understanding and knowledge of Scripture, we live in complete chaos and confusion... we do not know the music, but we do the best we can... we sing off key or in the wrong places... we confuse those around us, who have the music sheets, while we wander aimlessly in the dark, ruining things and making mistakes.

Why Scripture is so Important
The Bible tells us very clearly how to live, in every area of

life, without guessing, without singing incorrectly, without hurting and confusing ourselves and those around us, and without living in unnecessary pain, which we are guaranteed to do without the Blueprint. There is a large, deep chasm that separates us from God, and without knowing how to cross that chasm, we suffer in pain. We can only cross it, of course, through Jesus, but we cannot possibly know Jesus without His Word. Ignorance is no excuse. Lack of knowledge is a sin, for Scripture says, "My people are destroyed for lack of knowledge" (Hosea 4:6). We unknowingly destroy ourselves and others through our lack of knowledge and our ignorance of the Blueprint God gave us for life.

In the book of Judges, people did the best they could, without a Blueprint (even though they had one — the Law), and they did not follow Scripture. The book of Judges is a terribly violent book that describes the awful lives of people who continually sinned and infuriated God because, as the book ends, "All the people did what was right in their own eyes" (Judges 21:25). They did not use the sheet music, but they lived in the spirit of the music, which was their own "religion." Many of the people in Judges came to ruin as they hurt themselves and destroyed those around them.

The author of the book of Hebrews wrote, "Indeed, the word of God is living and active, sharper than any two-edged sword, piercing until it divides soul from spirit, joints from marrow; it is able to judge the thoughts and intentions of the heart" (Hebrews 4:12). We need the Word of God.

Shepherds and Sheep
Throughout Scripture, we can read how blind all of us are at times, and how many of us choose to remain blind, as if ignorance truly is bliss. God, who created us, knows how blind and senseless we often are. Because of our ignorance and fallen human nature, God gave us a Blueprint to read so

that we can use it to navigate through this life. The Blueprint (Scripture) is not a just rule-book, but is rather a wonderful gift given to us in order to protect and to guide us. Sheep need a shepherd. Sheep do not see very well; they could fall into a ditch and would be unable to climb out, and would lie there until they died from starvation, dehydration, exposure or consumption by another animal. Sheep wander away and get lost without a shepherd, just as we humans do. Isaiah 53:6 says, "All we like sheep have gone astray; we have all turned to our own way, and the Lord has laid on him the iniquity of us all." God knows that we need a Shepherd to guide us daily. Probably the most well-known Scripture that compares us to sheep and God to our shepherd is Psalm 23:

> "The Lord is my shepherd, I shall not want.
> He makes me lie down in green pastures.
> He leads me beside still waters;
> He restores my soul.
> He leads me in the paths of righteousness
> For His name's sake.
> Even though I walk through the valley
> Of the shadow of death
> I will fear no evil;
> For You are with me;
> Your rod and Your staff-
> They comfort me.
> You prepare a table before me
> In the presence of my enemies;
> You anoint my head with oil;
> My cup overflows.
> Surely goodness and mercy
> Shall follow me forever
> And I will dwell in the house of the Lord
> Forever."

Our Heavenly Father loves us so much and He longs to guide

and protect us, but for some reason, many of us do not think we need His help. Many want to wander away as sheep without a shepherd, and when they have fallen and cannot get up, or are being devoured by wolves, they wonder what went wrong. Jesus spoke so beautifully in John 10 about being our Shepherd:

> "Very truly, I tell you, anyone who does not enter the sheepfold by the gate but climbs in by another way is a thief and a bandit. The one who enters by the gate is the shepherd of the sheep. The gatekeeper opens the gate for him, and the sheep hear his voice, He calls for his own sheep by name and leads them out. When he has brought out all his own, he goes ahead of them, and the sheep follow him because they know his voice... I am the good shepherd. The good shepherd lays down his life for the sheep... I am the good shepherd. I know my own and my own know me, just as the Father knows me and I know the Father. And I lay down my life for the sheep."

There are numerous references in Scripture where Jesus compares us, His people, to sheep, and He is the Good Shepherd. Shepherds walk with their sheep and stay with them at all times in order to make sure they are safe; shepherds use a rod and a staff to bring their sheep back into safety when they are wandering into trouble or are too far away. Shepherds love, guide, protect, and care for their sheep. People, like sheep, need protection.

At the Grand Canyon, there are fences in place to keep visitors from falling to their deaths. Do you get angry that there are rules prohibiting people from climbing over these fences and plunging to their deaths? Does it not make sense to put barriers in place for safety? What about guardrails on highways, or crossing gates at train tracks? Do those safety measures or "rules" make you angry and want to rebel? God's

Word is no different, but is in place for our safety. The Good Shepherd wants to keep us safe and He does not want any of His sheep to perish.

Rules

Human nature is rebellious and generally does not like rules. Those who do not understand the teachings of Jesus Christ think Christianity is nothing but a set of arbitrary rules to follow that were put in place to ruin all of our fun. Christianity is so much richer and deeper than a set of meaningless rules. The Christian Faith is a wonderfully intimate relationship with the Creator of the universe, the God who loves us and even knows the number of hairs on our heads (Luke 12:7). I have often heard the saying, "Christianity is not about rules; it's about relationship"; but what loving relationship exists without rules? Just imagine if there were no rules to marriage. The Bible calls the followers of Christ His "Bride." Think about it. What if one spouse wanted to define "marriage" one way, but the other spouse wanted a different definition? — and what if the definition of "marriage" was considered by both spouses to be subjective? Marriage is defined as a monogamous relationship between one man and one woman, for life. What if the wife told her husband that her idea of marriage was to sleep with as many men as she would like, and that she had no obligations to her husband? The result would be painful. Marriage vows, in and of themselves, are rules that husbands and wives establish between one another for their own benefit and out of mutual love and respect. Such rules are to maintain a couple's fun, not to ruin a couple's fun. Divorce generally occurs when at least one party breaks the vows or "rules" of the marriage covenant. What relationship exists without rules? "Relationships" that have no rules are soon dissolved. Therefore, rules are a necessary component of all relationships. However, arbitrary rules do not enhance relationships. The Bible's rules are not arbitrary, but they are for our own good, and they stem from God's love. The Bible's rules are not a set of meaningless commands that inhibit life; rather, the Bible's rules are a set of meaningful commands that enrich life. We are to follow the teachings of Jesus and the commandments of God out of a deep love and desire to please Him.

Someone once told me that they did not think they could follow all the "rules" in the Bible, and therefore did not even bother to read it. He said he simply could not live "according to Scripture." The truth is that none of us can on our own. First of all, following Jesus is not about adhering to a strict set of *arbitrary* rules. Following Jesus is about loving God and loving your neighbor as yourself; that's it. Secondly, the only way we can even love like God commands us to love is through the power of the Holy Spirit, which Jesus promises us. No one can perfectly love and follow the very difficult, yet loving, teachings of Jesus on his or her own without the power of God.

In attempting to explain the Christian faith, the teachings of Jesus and the "rules" of the Bible, I sometimes compare Scripture to something I used to love to do — skydive. The first time a person jumps out of a perfectly good airplane, that person needs to have some training and the proper equipment. The main item that a skydiver needs is the parachute, but another very important piece of equipment is the altimeter, which is an instrument usually strapped onto one's wrist that displays the skydivers' altitude. The skydiver generally jumps at 13,500 feet, and free-falls until 5,500 feet, when it is time to pull the rip-cord that releases the parachute. While free-falling at 120 miles per hour, the skydiver cannot guess when she is at 5,500 feet, but she needs a gauge to tell her exactly when the correct and safe time to stop free-falling is, to slow down and to start floating under the safety and beauty of an open parachute. The altimeter is like the skydivers' Scripture (so to speak). The altimeter is an exact blueprint and gauge for safety, and it is in place literally to preserve one's life!

Without a gauge, the skydiver would be unbelievably lost and confused, unable to determine where she is, and perhaps would plummet to her death.

An example of the "rules" of Scripture that God commands us to follow is the Ten Commandments, which are "rules" to live by, as protective measures. For instance, the commandment, "Thou shall not murder" is for our protection. "Thou shall not steal" protects homes, families, and possessions. "Thou shall not commit adultery" is said out of love so others do not get hurt. All of the statutes or "rules," if you will, in the Bible, are all commanded by God to protect people from self-inflicted and unnecessary pain.

In his letter to the Romans, Paul wrote,
> "Owe no one anything, except to love one another; for the one who loves another has fulfilled the law. The commandments, 'You shall not commit adultery; You shall not murder; You shall not steal; You shall not covet'; and any other commandment, are summed up in this word, 'Love your neighbor as yourself.' Love does no wrong to a neighbor; therefore, love is the fulfilling of the law" (Romans 13:8-10).

The Law on our Heart
While God does indeed set up boundaries for our own good and protection, Christianity is not about adhering to a strict set of *arbitrary* rules, but it is about a relationship with Jesus and a way of life that ultimately sets us free. Christians live according to Scripture because they have a longing for God and only want to do what pleases Him. God said,

> "The days are surely coming, says the Lord,
> When I will establish a new covenant
> With the house of Israel
> And with the house of Judah;

> Not like the covenant that I made
> With their ancestors,
> On the day when I took them by the hand
> To lead them out of the land of Egypt;
> For they did not continue in my covenant,
> And so I had no concern for them,
> Says the Lord.
> This is the covenant that I will make
> With the house of Israel
> After those days, says the Lord:
> I will put my laws in their minds,
> And write them on their hearts,
> And I will be their God,
> And they shall be my people.
> And they shall not teach one another
> Or say to each other, 'Know the Lord,'
> For they shall all know me,
> From the least of them to the greatest.
> For I will be merciful toward their iniquities,
> And I will remember their sins no more."
>
> Hebrews 8:8-12

Christians (Christ-followers, who know the Bible and Jesus personally) do not follow Scripture because we read the "rules" and perceive a compulsion to obey, lest we feel guilty or afraid. Christians follow the teachings of Jesus and the commands of God because we WANT to, because we love Him, and because He wrote them on our hearts. God gives us the desire to follow and obey Him. If you do not have a burning, longing and desire to obey Scripture, you probably do not know Jesus.

If you have a spouse or a sweetheart, or if you have parents, friends or children whom you love, do you not want to do what pleases those people? If you love someone, you naturally want to do the things that you know make that person happy, and you want to avoid any words and actions that you know irritate, disrespect, or hurt that person. Loving is all about relationship. If you love Jesus, all you want to do is glorify, please, honor, and love Him through your words and actions. The whole Law is summed up in this command: Love God and love your neighbor as yourself. If you love, you will want to obey; however, no one, including Jesus, ever said it would be easy.

Scripture and Temptations
In Luke 4, Satan attempted to tempt Jesus in the wilderness for forty days. Jesus had not eaten for those forty days and was obviously quite hungry when Satan approached Him. Satan told the famished Jesus, "If you are the Son of God, command this stone to become a loaf of bread" (Luke 4:3). Jesus quoted part of Deuteronomy 8, when He said to Satan in response to the first temptation, "It is written, 'One does not live by bread alone...'" The entire passage, which Satan would have known, was spoken to the Israelites on their way into the Promised Land. It says,

> "This entire commandment that I command you today you must diligently observe, so that you may live and increase, and go in and occupy the land that the Lord promised on oath to your ancestors. Remember the long way that the Lord your God has led you these forty years in the wilderness, in order to humble you, testing to know what was in your heart, whether or not you would keep His commandments. He humbled you by letting you hunger, then by feeding you with manna, which neither you nor your ancestors were acquainted, in order to make you understand that one does not live by bread alone, but by every word that comes from the mouth of the Lord" (Deuteronomy 8:1-3).

Satan knew Jesus was starving, so he tried to tempt Him with food. It is when we are most vulnerable that Satan attacks, and the mightiest tool we have is the tool Jesus used — Scripture. Jesus relied on Scripture for the next two trials as well, as He did for the remainder of His ministry.

The second time Satan tried to tempt Jesus, when the devil told Jesus to worship him, Jesus responded again by quoting Deuteronomy 6:13-14: "It is written, 'Worship the Lord your God, and serve only him'" (Luke 4:8). Satan's third and last endeavor to tempt Christ was for Jesus to prove He was the Son of God by throwing Himself from the highest point of the Temple so that God would send His angels to rescue Him. Satan then quoted Scripture (imperfectly) to Jesus: "He will order his angels to be responsible for you and to protect you. They will support you with their hands, so that you will not hurt your feet on the stones" (Psalm 91:11-12). Satan conveniently omitted that the angels would guard Him in all His ways, and then Satan, of course, did not continue with the next verse which reads, "You will tread on the lion and the adder, the young lion and the serpent you will trample under foot," which Christ does to Satan! Even Satan knows the power of God's Word, which he attempted to use to tempt Jesus, and which Jesus quoted in return to defeat Satan. If Jesus, the Son of God knows the power of Scripture, and the highest created being, Lucifer (now Satan), is also aware of this power, why do humans avoid harnessing this same power? Many people take the Bible so lightly, and perhaps only read it when they have nothing else to do, for they do not make it priority. How much more power could we live in daily if we were able to quote Scripture to Satan when he tempts us or when we are feeling weak and vulnerable?

Jesus understands temptation, but He never sinned; "For we do not have a high priest who is unable to sympathize with our weaknesses, but we have one who in every respect has been tested as we are, yet without sin" (Hebrews 4:15). In the midst of His trials, the very first words that Jesus spoke were, "It is written..." (Luke 4:4). The one thing that drove Satan away from Jesus was the Word of God, i.e. Scripture. Jesus told Satan that we are to live "...by every word that comes from the mouth of the Lord." How do we live as the Gospel commands us to live? The Lord's Words are found in Scripture, so Jesus must have therefore meant that we are to live according to Scripture.

Paul knew the importance of the Word of God, in all of life's trials and temptations, when he wrote about spiritual warfare and standing against Satan in Ephesians 6:10-17:

> "Finally, be strong in the Lord and in the strength of his power. Put on the whole armor of God, so that you may be able to stand against the wiles of the devil. For our struggle is not against enemies of blood and flesh, but against the rulers, against the authorities, against the cosmic powers of this present darkness, against the spiritual forces of evil in the heavenly places. Therefore take up the whole armor of God, so that you may be able to withstand on that evil day, and having done everything to stand firm. Stand therefore, and fasten the belt of truth around your waist and put on the breastplate of righteousness. As shoes for your feet put on whatever will make you ready to proclaim the gospel of peace. With all of these, take the shield of faith, with which you will be able to quench all the flaming arrows of the evil one. Take the helmet of salvation, and the sword of the Spirit, **which is the word of God.**"

If Jesus, the Son of God, relied on Scripture when He was tried by Satan (though Jesus never sinned), how much more should we, whose hearts are "fully set... to do evil" (Ecclesiastes 8:11) rely on the Bible? How can we rely on Scripture and quote it back to Satan as Jesus did if we do not know it?

Living Without Confusion

Where do we find the word of the Lord to live by? — Scripture. God wants us to stop wandering in the wilderness and to enter into His Promised Land. Look at a map of where the Israelites wandered for forty years; it did not require forty years to cross that desert (geographically) in order to *begin* their stay in the Promised Land, so it should not take people their entire lives to *begin* walking with God. In fact, in the Book of Genesis, Joseph's brothers traveled back and forth along the very same stretch of land several times within a relatively brief period (certainly nothing like forty years). Many of us wander aimlessly for forty years or more because we do not use the map, the Blueprint, and we disobey our Savior by refusing to make Him our Lord and our Guide. We just want to do the best we can, enjoy our free gift of salvation, get into Heaven by the skin of our teeth (with no eternal rewards), and never experience the abundant life Jesus promised when we live according to His Word, and in the power of God. Life passes us by, with the Blueprint on our shelves, as we suffer needlessly, while dragging others with us through the mire.

Jesus, a carpenter, used a building analogy when He spoke about our faith. He said in Luke 14:27-28 & 33, "Whoever does not carry the cross and follow Me cannot be my disciple. For which of you, intending to build a tower, does not first sit down and estimate the cost, to see whether he has enough to complete it?... So therefore, none of you can become my disciple if you do not give up all your possessions." Being a Christian is not going through the motions, singing songs, performing rituals, praying once in a while and going to church on Sunday. A Christian sacrificially loves God and all people, in pure loyalty, honesty, and devotion. Do not take my word for it; look for yourself — it is all right there, in the Blueprint, the Bible.

With a lifetime of avoiding Scripture, we begin to realize we were lost.

"If you keep my commandments, you will abide in my love, just as I have kept my Father's commandments and abide in His love. I have said these things to you so that my joy may be in you, and that your joy may be complete."

(John 15:10-11)

CHAPTER FOUR

The Grace of God

Safety in Grace
All of us want joy in our lives. All of us want to feel safe. All of us want to feel loved and protected. God is fully aware of those needs that are in us since He made us. Through our obedience to Him, the grace of God will not only **cause** us to feel safe, loved and protected, but we **WILL,** in reality, be safe, loved and protected **because** of God's grace. Some people view God as primarily vengeful because they do not understand grace. Perhaps we do not understand grace because we do not live in it ourselves. Perhaps we do not understand grace because Satan is incredibly clever and deceitful, and he distorts our ideas of God's love, grace, and protection. I have even heard some people say that they think God is a hateful God because He gives us a lot of rules to follow, and when we break these rules, we fall under His wrath and anger. Who could love and serve a God who is just waiting to strike us down? Actually, no one could love such a God, but Scripture says that God is love (1 John 4:16). Do God's "rules" show Him to be a God of love and compassion, or a God of hate?

As in all of Satan's deceptions, there is always a grain of truth in order to deceive. When we do not live under God's laws, we are indeed under His anger and wrath, but only because He is a God of such great and perfect love. God is called our Father throughout Scripture, and what loving Father does not have rules for his children to follow for their own protection? If you are a parent, do you hate your young children because you do not allow them to play in the middle of the street? If you see your child run into the street, do you not discipline him in some way so he will learn and know not to do that again because it is so dangerous? Do you hate your teenage daughter because you do not allow her out at all hours of the night? If you discovered that she did indeed sneak out late at night, would you not discipline or punish her in some way as well? Do you hate your children because you discipline them, or do you discipline them out of love? We all seem to understand that parents establish rules and boundaries for their children out of love and protection. In a similar way, God our Father established His rules and boundaries for us, His children, in the world that He created; however, it, somehow, is often difficult to understand a similar parental concept of love with respect to God. Instead, many view God as a God of anger, wrath, and hate. Why is that?

Hebrews 12: 5-11 states:

> "My child, do not regard lightly the discipline of the Lord, or lose heart when you are punished by him; for the Lord disciplines those whom he loves, and chastises every child whom he accepts. Endure trials for the sake of discipline. God is treating you as children; for what child is there whom a parent does not discipline? If you do not have that discipline in which all children share, then you are illegitimate and not his children. Moreover, we had human parents to discipline us, and we respected them. Should we not even be more willing to be subject to the Father of spirits and live? For they disciplined us for a short time as seemed best to them, but he disciplines

us for our good, in order that we may share in his holiness. Now, discipline always seems painful rather than pleasant at the time, but later it yields the peaceful fruit of righteousness to those who have been trained by it."

God sets His "rules" or boundaries, His Blueprint for us, just as any loving parent does for his children… for our safety, our protection, and for our own good. David wrote, in Psalm 119:97-98, "Oh, how I love your law! It is my meditation all day long. Your commandment makes me wiser than my enemies, for it is always with me." Being wiser than our enemies is an advantage that only someone who loves us and desires to keep us safe would want us to have.

What Exactly is the Bible?
Many people who are unfamiliar with the Bible think it is an old, outdated book full of a bunch of rules that either no longer apply or that most people merely do not want to follow; how sad such a misperception truly is! Those who have read the Bible cover-to-cover many times see it as something much different. The Bible is not only the greatest piece of literature ever written, filled with history, drama, poetry, letters, and beauty, but it is a book about complete and total freedom in Christ, and about God's love, mercy, and grace. Many who have not studied Scripture often believe that God is merely some abstract concept or Being whom we could never begin to understand, and such people would be surprised that the Bible states otherwise. The Bible beautifully paints a description of what God is like through the life-stories of the people who are recorded in Scripture, and through the life of Jesus Christ (who was God in human flesh). If we read the Bible, then we can actually begin to know God personally, which is what God deeply desires, and we cannot help but fall deeply in love with Him.

Throughout the entire Bible, we read about failure after failure of human beings, from the greatest to the least. We read about such great people as Moses, Noah, Abraham, Joseph, King David, Solomon, and all of the Apostles, including Paul, who each failed miserably, yet God continued to love them. Each time one of these people fell and sinned, after they repented, God forgave them and had restorative plans for their lives, including their ultimate salvation. The Bible is basically a book about the amazing love and grace of God, displayed over and over, despite human failure that is committed over and over.

You are What You Eat
How does reading the Bible daily, studying God's Word, and living according to Scripture actually make a difference in who we are? How can learning to read the Blueprint change our lives? What do the words in the Bible have to do with day-to-day living? — Everything. The Bible was never meant to be a part of our lives that we read in our spare time, but it was given to us to become our actual, daily lives. God commanded the Old Testament prophet Ezekiel to eat the scroll, or the words of God;

> "But you, mortal, hear what I say to you; do not be rebellious like that rebellious house; open your mouth and eat what I give you.' I looked, and a hand was stretched out to me, and a written scroll was in it. He spread it before me; it had writing on the front and on the back, and written on it were words of lamentation and mourning and woe. He said to me, 'O mortal, eat what is offered to you; eat this scroll, and go, speak to the house of Israel.' So I opened my mouth, and he gave me the scroll to eat. He said to me, 'Mortal, eat this scroll that I give you and fill your stomach with it.' Then I ate it; and in my mouth it was as sweet as honey"
> (Ezekiel 2:8-10 & 3:1-3).

Did Ezekiel actually eat a paper scroll which tasted like honey, or is this passage of Scripture a metaphor for ingesting God's Word, which is as sweet as honey? There is that saying, "You are what you eat," which means that what you eat basically becomes a part of you. If we "eat" God's Word, the idea is that Scripture will become a part of us as we ingest its sweetness. Perhaps this ingesting of Scripture is what David was referring to in Psalm 23 when he wrote, "You prepare a table before me in the presence of my enemies; you anoint my head with oil; my cup overflows. Surely goodness and mercy shall follow me all the days of my life, and I shall dwell in the house of the Lord forever." We can become one with Scripture. Read, ingest, and enjoy God's Word so that the blessings David mentions will also be yours. There is safety and power in God's Word, and He spreads His Word out before us, offering the satisfaction that only a life lived for Him through His Word can bring. The problem is that many of us live in Scriptural ignorance, basically because of laziness and apathy to the very words of God. We therefore miss out on a rich, full life, and instead are satisfied with blindness.

A Picture of God
The Bible is divided into the Old and the New Testaments, making the Bible one complete, Holy book. I have heard countless Christians say they do not read the Old Testament because it "no longer applies"; I have no idea what that statement means. It no longer applies to what? What no longer applies? While it is true that we are, "not under law but under grace" (Romans 6:14), Jesus said, "Do not think that I have come to abolish the law or the prophets; I have come not to abolish but to fulfill" (Matthew 5:17). Should we therefore not be familiar with what it is that Jesus fulfilled, and how? What exactly is the law, who are the prophets? — Jesus is referring to the Old Testament books. They were important to Him, yet they are not recognized as being important to so many Christ-followers. How can we possibly understand what

Jesus was doing and fulfilling, if we do not know to what He is referring? Can we understand Jesus without the knowledge of what it was He said He came to Earth to do?

The Old Testament is filled with fascinating stories of the lives of so many people who both loved and served God, and of those who did not. Through these stories, told in great detail, we see the hand of God move, and we get a detailed picture of who God is, how He works, and we can begin to understand His nature, even in our finite minds. Many people do not know God and cannot ever see Him in their lives because they do not know how to recognize Him; they cannot hear Him since they are unfamiliar with Scripture, which is God's voice.

The Old Testament
The Old Testament is composed of twenty-four books, sectioned into three divisions: The Law or Pentateuch (the first five books of the Bible), The Prophets (consisting of Former and Latter Prophets, in eight books) and the Writings (eleven books), which includes the Wisdom Literature. The Bible begins with the book of Genesis, which gives the story of creation and the first sin, which subsequently brought about death.

From the very beginning of the Bible, in the book of Genesis, we witness the mistakes, the **sins** (a word which not many use anymore) of humanity and the mess it made in the Garden of Eden. More importantly, we see God immediately show His love and mercy after that first sin. God banished Adam and Eve from the Garden — out of grace — because they could still eat from the Tree of Life and live forever, though in a fallen, sinful state. Would you want to live forever on earth with sickness, pain, disease and sorrow? God also had a plan for our salvation from the time of that very first sin, which is only found in the death and resurrection of Jesus Christ. The Bible tells us that God saw our sin, yet He loved us so much that He refused to let us go. Throughout the Bible, the truth of God's love is narrated through stories, letters, historical narratives, parables, poetry, and in the life of Jesus.

God's Lament
"The Lord saw that the wickedness of humankind was great in the earth, and that every inclination of the thoughts of their hearts was only evil continually. And the Lord was sorry that he had made humankind on the earth, and it grieved him to his heart" (Genesis 6:5 - 6). God had the option and ability to destroy humans forever, but in His grace and love, He saved a remnant — Noah and his family, who loved God and wanted to obey Him. God gave humanity another chance because of His grace. After the flood waters receded, God said, "I will never again curse the ground because of humankind, for the inclination of the human heart is evil from youth" (Genesis 8:21). One of the saddest verses in the Bible, in my opinion, that relates to this Old Testament verse is found in the Gospel of John in the New Testament; "But Jesus on his part would not entrust himself to them, because he knew all people and needed no one to testify about anyone; for he himself knew what was in everyone" (John 2:24-25). God knows humankind is evil, yet He still loves us and forgives us and is always with us, promising to never leave or forsake us (Hebrews 13:5). God gave His Holy Word to help us on our journey and keep us safe.

Covenants and Law
The Bible conveys, over and over again, that God did indeed set His law for our safety and protection, just like earthly parents, through His covenant with us. The Old Testament book of Deuteronomy emphasizes God's covenantal protection for us through His love and is described as, "the reaffirmation of the covenant between God and the people of Israel" (The New Oxford Annotated Bible, 217). A covenant is defined by Webster's dictionary as, "a written agreement or promise,

under seal between two or more parties especially for the performance of some action." What might this action be, and who is involved in the covenant God made with us? God said,

> "The days are surely coming, says the Lord, when I will make a new covenant with the house of Israel and the house of Judah. It will not be like the covenant that I made with their ancestors when I took them by the hand to bring them out of the land of Egypt — a covenant that they broke, though I was their husband, says the Lord; I will put my law within them, and I will write it on their hearts; and I will be their God, and they shall be my people. No longer shall they teach one another, or say to each other, 'Know the Lord,' for they shall all know me, from the least of them to the greatest, says the Lord; for I will forgive their iniquity, and remember their sin no more" (Jeremiah 31:31-34).

God's covenant is with all those who faithfully love and obey Him and keep His covenant. Like a marriage covenant, God's covenant with us stems from His sacrificial love for us, and is put in place to keep us safe and protected, as a husband does (or should do) for his wife. We who follow Jesus and obey His commands are the "Bride of Christ" according to the Bible in Revelation 21:9, and God, our husband, protects us and keeps us safe in His love.

"Know therefore that the Lord your God is God, the faithful God who maintains covenant loyalty with those who love him and keep his commandments, to a thousand generations" (Deuteronomy 7:9). God desires to be our Father, our husband, our God, who loves and protects us, and all He wants in return is for us to acknowledge that love and to love Him back. How do we love God? Again, Scripture defines this love: Jesus said we love Him if we obey His commands (John 14:15) which are not burdensome, but a delightful protection of love.

For Our Own Well-being

In the book of Deuteronomy, God told Moses to tell the Israelites to keep His statutes and commandments, "for your own well-being" (Deuteronomy 4:40). God also said, "You must follow exactly the path the Lord your God has commanded you, so that you may live and that it may go well with you" (Deuteronomy 5:33). God also said, "What does the Lord require of you? Only to fear the Lord your God, to walk in all his ways, to love him, to serve the Lord your God with all your heart and with all your soul, and to keep the commandments of the Lord your God and his decrees that I am commanding you today, for your own well-being" (Deuteronomy 10:12-13). Again, "Be careful to obey all these words that I command you today, so that it may go well with you and your children after you forever, because you will be doing what is good and right in the sight of the Lord your God" (Deuteronomy 12:28). Why does God tell us to keep His commands and to follow His Blueprint for life? – **FOR OUR OWN WELL-BEING!** He is trying to protect us. He is trying to show His love for us. He is trying to keep us safe.

Deuteronomy 11:26-28 says, "See, I am setting before you today a blessing and a curse: the blessing if you obey the commandments of the Lord your God that I am commanding you today; and the curse if you do not obey the commandments of the Lord your God, but turn away from the way that I am commanding you today."

It is never too late to obtain God's blessings. When the Israelites had disobeyed God and turned away from His Word and commands, God said to them, "Return to the Lord your God, and you and your children obey him with all your heart and with all your soul, just as I am commanding you today, then the Lord your God will restore your fortunes and have compassion on you" (Deuteronomy 30:2-3). "For the Lord will again take delight in prospering you, just as he delighted in prospering your ancestors when you obey the Lord your God by observing his commandments and decrees that are written in this book of the law, because you turn to the Lord your God with all your heart and with all your soul" (Deuteronomy 30:9b-10). God's grace is always available to us because of His great love for us. Does this sound like a God of harshness, or a God of love? Does this God sound like a Father who longs for good things for His children, or a Father who does not care for his children and has no desire to protect them?

The Prophets
The Prophetic books were written to convey God's message through the voices of the various prophets who spoke of God's judgment, often to entire nations who refused to listen, and of God's salvation and restoration to those who would indeed listen. Many of the prophetic messages concerned God's judgment and anger at disobedient and complacent people (like today's lukewarm Christians) and of their failure to live according to Scripture. The prophets spoke harshly, in the name of Yahweh, in order to bring people to repentance and to live in obedience to God's Word. Each time the prophets were ignored, God's righteous judgment did eventually fall on the people who refused to listen, since they failed to live in the manner God designed for them to live in, according to His perfect plan. Whenever the people did acknowledge the prophets' words and live according to the Blueprint God clearly laid out, God restored them, blessed them, and helped them walk out of confusion and into a life of clarity and wisdom.

While the prophets lived hundreds of years before Christ, their message remains true today; God is angered by those who refuse to read, study, and live according to His Word. People who refuse to follow and submit to Christ will surely live in chaos, confusion, and blindness, to their eventual destruction. On the other hand, God is merciful and full of love, and He is always ready to forgive and restore when we turn from our self-serving and complacent ways, and learn to submit, love, and serve Him. The writers of the Bible did not record the words of the prophets for historical fact only, but like the entire Bible, the prophets' words and messages are given for our current understanding as well, so that we may live wisely and learn from the past. The prophets consistently warned the people that living on our own, outside of the parameters of God's Word, is simply not a wise option!

Wisdom
The entire Bible is filled with advice, commands, and illustrations to help us navigate our way through life, page by page, like a Blueprint. "Whoever heeds instruction is on the path to life" (Proverbs 10:17). The Old Testament Wisdom books provide the reader with wise counsel and moral sayings or maxims to live by through allegory, poetry, songs, stories, and proverbs. The theme of wisdom in Scripture is to aid us in interpreting the Bible theologically, through past and present life experience, with a reverent fear of the Lord. "When the Bible speaks of 'wisdom,' it is talking about cleverness or instrumental skill, about human moral judgment, about a quest to live in harmony with the order of creation, or about a prudence incorporating all of the above *after* beginning with the 'fear of the Lord'" (Daniel Treier, in Dictionary for Theological Interpretation, 844).

Many of us read through the Wisdom books quickly, rather than meditate on them and understand what God wants to teach us through each message. The first chapter of Proverbs states that, "The fear of the Lord is the beginning of knowledge; fools despise wisdom and instruction" (Proverbs 1:7). To fear the Lord means to have a healthy reverence and awe of Him as the Creator of the Universe, as the Author and Giver of Life, as the One who has full control over all matters, including when and how we live, and when and how we die. When we do not live according to Scripture, we do not live in the fear of the Lord. When we live in obedience to Scripture, we live with character, since we then live in wisdom rather than in foolishness... or what Scripture calls, "folly" (Treier, 845). Wisdom, as found in Scripture, teaches us to live in harmony with the created order of God's world and to avoid the difficult consequences of sin.

God lovingly gives us some of His wisdom, recorded in Scripture, for our own good, as the book of Deuteronomy repeatedly states, and as the Bible also promises, with both blessings and curses. Proverbs 1:33 says, "But those who listen to me will be secure and will live at ease, without dread of disaster." Christians can live in ease not because we will avoid life's problems, but because we will be in the center of God's will and understand we are safe within His reach. Why would humans neglect the vast, incomprehensible wisdom of God, which He offers through His Word? God does indeed want good things for His people. God wants us to live in joy, in safety, in wisdom, and in grace. We can learn a great deal of how to live wisely through the wisdom books given to us in the Old Testament; but in order to live wisely, we must read Scripture!

The Cohesiveness of Scripture
In the New Testament, we read about the life of Jesus. Jesus is God in the flesh, and His life enables us to have a further understanding of who God is. However, Jesus often referred to the Old Testament Scriptures and used Old Testament imagery in His stories; so, in order to appreciate fully and to understand Jesus and His teachings in the New Testament, we do need to have an understanding and a knowledge of the Old Testament. We need to be very familiar with the entire Bible if we are to call ourselves Christ-followers and claim to have a relationship with God. One cannot pick up a book 2/3 of the way through and claim to understand the characters and how the story ends! Like a blueprint, we need each

page to see the final building. The Old Testament comes to fulfillment in Jesus Christ, as is recorded in each book of the New Testament.

The New Testament
The New Testament contains twenty-seven books, arranged into four sections: The Gospels, The Acts of the Apostles, the Letters, and the Apocalypse, or the book of Revelation. God's New Covenant is fulfilled and explained in the life of Jesus and the gift of the Holy Spirit, given to those who accept Jesus as their Lord and Savior. Those people who have the Holy Spirit are then given the power and ability to understand the Blueprint for life, how to read it, and how to live in its Truth.

Because God loves us more than we will ever comprehend, He chooses to redeem us from our selfishness and sin. He restored His relationship with us by becoming one of us, a human, in order for us to be reconciled to Him, to know Him, and to have a deep, personal relationship with Him. The way God redeems us is recorded in the New Testament, where God became man and taught us the Blueprint for life.

The Life of Jesus
The word "gospel" means "good news." We have the good news of our salvation through Jesus Christ, both in eternity and also as we live out our lives here on earth, IF we live according to Scripture. The Gospels (Matthew, Mark, Luke, and John) give accounts of the life of Jesus Christ who was God in human flesh. People sinned and, as a result, separated themselves from God. In order for God to save people from their separation from Him, He chose to become one of us and to experience humanity in all of its brokenness, frailty, and weakness. As a man, Jesus lived without ever sinning. Jesus experienced humanity fully, yet He never gave in to any temptation. He lived a perfect life: "For we do not have a high priest who is unable to sympathize with our weaknesses, but

we have one who in every respect has been tested as we are, yet without sin" (Hebrews 4:15).

The Gospels give us an account of the life, the ministry, and the teachings of Jesus, as well as His death and His resurrection. Through the life of Jesus, we can gain an understanding of God's character and how we are supposed to think and live. Christians are called to be imitators of Jesus Christ. If we do not know who He is, what He says, how He thinks, and how He lived on earth, then how can we know how to imitate Him? Therefore, if we call ourselves Christians, then obviously we must read Scripture in order to know Jesus and to live according to His will and plans for our lives. The Church is called the "Bride" of Christ. Who would think of maintaining a marital relationship without listening to, speaking with, learning about, or serving his or her own spouse? How then can people call themselves "Christians," who constitute the "Bride," without listening to the message of God's Word and the life of Jesus as written in the Gospels?

The First Christian Church — Acts
The book of Acts is a continuation of the Gospel of Luke. Acts shows us that God is the One in control — not us, even though some people like to think they are. Acts talks about how the first Christian church was formed and of the many missionary journeys of the Apostle Paul whose work started numerous churches in the ancient world. God was, and always will be, the One in full control, who moves people around to accomplish His will. If one chooses to ignore God and His will, then He will find someone else to do His work, and that person will miss out on much of life. God has a purpose, which is for all to love and to serve Him and others, to live a life submitted to His Word, and to guide and direct us in order to bring others to His saving love. In order for God to do this work through us, we must be able to hear His voice, which is heard through Scripture.

Paul started churches solely on the basis of Scripture, which, in his day, was the Old Testament. In the book of Acts, Paul repeatedly proved the case for Christ through the use of Scripture, which he basically had memorized; "From morning till evening he explained and declared to them the kingdom of God and tried to convince them about Jesus from the Law of Moses and from the Prophets," (Acts 28:23). The New Testament did not yet exist when Paul founded churches. Scripturally, Paul relied entirely on the Old Testament to explain Christ. Had Paul not made Scripture (the Old Testament) part of his daily life, he would not have had the necessary resources to explain Christ. Through the quotation of Acts (above), we can see that most of the people to whom Paul spoke did not have a thorough knowledge of the Old Testament — even the religious elites! Paul inadvertently wrote much of the New Testament by proving Christ from the Old Testament; this should tell us that, without consistently studying the Old Testament, we have no way to understand who Christ is, as was the case when Paul taught. Without a thorough knowledge of Scripture, the Church could have never even begun and cannot continue.

Letters
The New Testament Letters were written with specific instructions for people to live the Christian life and for churches to function correctly as the Body of Christ, just as a Blueprint is written to instruct builders how to build correctly for a solid, finished product. Scripture often uses various aspects of familial relations to teach us how we are to relate to God and to each other. In one of the Letters, Christians are compared to children in relation to God; "Everyone who believes that Jesus is the Christ has been born of God, and everyone who loves the parent loves the child. By this we know that we love God and obey his commandments. For the love of God is this, that we obey his commandments. And his commandments are not burdensome." (1 John 5:2-3)

The Bible tells us how to love God and that we cannot love God if we do not follow His commandments. However, we cannot follow His commandments if we do not read His Word. Therefore, if one calls oneself a Christian, then one must read Scripture in order to understand God's commandments which, in turn, tell us how to love God. The Letters reinforce God's protective love for us when we live according to Scripture. The Bible is reciprocal. God loves us and He therefore gave us commandments for our own good, which "are not burdensome"; if we, for our own good, keep God's commandments, we then prove our love for God.

Revelation
The Bible ends with the book of Revelation, which tells of the final battle between good and evil where good prevails, of course. The book of Revelation was written by the Apostle John when he was an old man. Revelation is the Apocalypse. According to the *Critical Lexicon and Concordance to the English and Greek New Testament*, by E.W. Bullinger, "αποκαλυψις *revelation*" means "unveiling, uncovering: *of facts and truths,* disclosure, revelation; *of persons,* appearing, manifestation"; the dictionary entry's note further states that, "The book so called, relates all the facts and circumstances and judgments attending the Second Coming, *or* revelation, *or* appearing of the Lord Jesus Christ."

The book of Revelation tells us plainly that Jesus is coming back. He will hold us all accountable for our words and actions. We can learn how to speak and act as God requires only through Scripture, which is why God gave us His Word in the first place. Not reading, knowing, or living according to Scripture will not be an excuse. Jesus said, "Behold, I am coming soon! My reward is with me, and I will give to everyone according to what he has done" (Revelation 22:12). The book of Revelation, and subsequently the entire Bible, ends with the words of Jesus who says, "Yes, I am coming soon. Amen.

Come, Lord Jesus. The grace of the Lord Jesus be with the God's people. Amen." Will you be ready?

The Problem with the Church
Scripture is written for us to understand, but it is not subject to individual interpretation. II Peter 1:20 states, "No Scripture is of any private interpretation." Scripture, when read thoroughly, is actually quite clear, and it interprets itself. One example that I have often heard is a strange controversy about why Sodom and Gomorrah were destroyed; the story is found in Genesis 19. I once heard a pastor say these cities were destroyed for a lack of hospitality. The God in Scripture does not rain down sulfur and fire from Heaven and destroy entire cities for a lack of hospitality! Am I making up the God I choose to believe in, or does Scripture actually tell us the reason for the destruction of Sodom and Gomorrah? If we are unfamiliar with the Bible, then we simply believe what we are told by our pastor, who must surely know what he is talking about… after all, he IS the pastor — Right? Or, we can actually read the Bible, which clearly tells us why these cities were destroyed. Many, many pages after Genesis, in the second-to-last book of the Bible (the book of Jude), Scripture states that, "Sodom and Gomorrah and the surrounding cities, which, in the same manner as they, indulged in sexual immorality and pursued unnatural lust, serve as an example by undergoing a punishment of eternal fire." Scripture, not a pastor, interprets Scripture.

Well, some may argue, what exactly defines "unnatural" lust/sexuality? Again, Scripture clearly defines "unnatural lust" in another area of the Bible, "For this reason God gave them up to degrading passions. Their women exchanged natural intercourse for unnatural, and in the same way also the men, giving up natural intercourse with women, were consumed with passion for one another. Men committed shameless acts with men and received in their own persons the due penalty for their error" (Romans 1:26-27). Sodom and Gomorrah were destroyed because of sexual immorality and homosexuality, not for a lack of hospitality. The misinterpretation of the Sodom and Gomorrah story is just one example of making up the "Christian faith" for lack of knowledge, which Scripture also addresses: "My people are destroyed for lack of knowledge" (Hosea 4:6). We humans are most certainly self-destructive!

The Unity of the Bible
The illustration above was given since it is a familiar story to most people who have a basic knowledge of Scripture, in order to show that the Bible is a perfectly uniform book which needs to be read as a whole. The Old Testament interprets the New Testament, and the New Testament interprets the Old Testament.

Some people will never recover the lives God intended for them because they fail to read the Bible and to find the answers to their questions about how to live. God never intended for us to stumble around like lost sheep without a shepherd, or like construction workers without a blueprint, or like musicians who cannot read music. God loves us far too much to leave us in one of those states. He provided us with His Word so that we can indeed know Him and His desire and plans for our lives.

Jesus corrected some of the most educated and religious people of His day who were trying to trap Him by implying He was wrong in His teachings and was contradicting Scripture; "Jesus answered them, 'You are wrong, because you know neither the scriptures nor the power of God'" (Matthew 22:29). Many place God in the box of their own making. Many believe they are good Christians, loving and pleasing God, while all along, in their chosen ignorance, they are infuriating Him. Many create idols, many break the Ten Commandments, many ignore the teachings of Jesus, and many live in sin and rebellion. Many believe God is with us at all times and hears our prayers, even though the Bible tells us God is not always in our midst, and does not hear our prayers when we live apart from Him. Many walk into church on Sunday, sing songs and lift their hands in praise to a God who does not even exist, but is one of their imaginations. Many feel good about themselves until the next Sunday, while they live like fools and hypocrites. No wonder the world hates Christians.

With a little inquiry and knowledge of Scripture, one begins to move in the right direction towards recovery.

PRACTICE

"All scripture is inspired by God and is useful for teaching, for reproof, for correction, and for training in righteousness, so that everyone who belongs to God may be proficient, equipped for every good work."

(2 Timothy 3:16-17)

CHAPTER FIVE

The Road to Recovery

Where to Begin
Recovery begins with the awareness and the realization that we are all lost and need help. When we begin to realize there is that something that is not quite right, and that we have gotten lost along the way, where do we even begin to find our path and start the recovery process? First of all, we must begin in complete humility, on our knees, understanding that we are in need and are blind, fumbling around in the dark, alone, and lost. We need a Savior. We need Jesus Christ. How do we find Him and know Him?

If we call out to God, He is there and will assuredly answer. Revelation 3:20 says, "Behold, I stand at the door and knock: If any man hear My voice, and open the door, I will come in." In order to hear Jesus and get to know Him, who He is, and to have an intimate relationship with Him, we need to read the Bible. When we read Scripture, we will find God and discover who He is, what He expects from us, how He wants us to live, and who we are meant to be.

Scripture
After acknowledging our need for Christ, the Messiah, we need to go to the Bible. We cannot even begin to know we are

lost or blind without the Scriptures. The apostle Paul wrote that unless we have the Law (the *Written* Law in Scripture), we do not even know that we break the law or are doing anything wrong! "For through the law comes the knowledge of sin" (Romans 3:20b). None of us are capable of following God's Law, as written in Scripture, which is why Jesus came to earth as a man and died for us.

Christianity is the only religion that fully understands human weakness, limitations, and shortcomings. We can never be good or holy enough to earn our salvation. The Christian faith teaches that eternal life and forgiveness of sins comes only through faith in Christ when we accept His gift of grace to us, rather than by earning our salvation through our own goodness, which is rather minimal. However, our inability to perfectly keep God's Law, and His love and forgiveness that follows our blunders, does not give us the freedom to sin. Many "Christians" think that God is *only* a God of love, mercy, grace, and forgiveness. God is loving, merciful, and forgiving, but just because He is good does not mean that we have license to sin. Such a misunderstanding of God's love is considered a heresy and is called antinomianism, which is strongly refuted throughout Scripture, especially by Paul:

> "For you were called to freedom, brothers and sisters; only do not use your freedom as an opportunity for self-indulgence, but through love become slaves to one another. For the whole law is summed up in a single commandment, 'You shall love your neighbor as yourself.'" (Galatians 5:13-14)

The New Testament book of James consistently explains that we are not to be merely hearers of the Word of God, but doers of the Word (Scripture). We are called to live out our faith by our actions:

> "What good is it, my brothers and sisters, if you say you have faith but do not have works? Can faith save you? If a brother or sister is naked and lacks daily food, and one of you says to them, 'Go in peace; keep warm and eat your fill,' and yet you do not supply their bodily needs, what is the good of that? So faith, if it has no works, is dead. But someone will say, 'Show me your faith apart from your works, and I by my works will show you my faith. You believe that God is one; you do well. Even the demons believe — and shudder. Do you want to be shown, you senseless person, that faith apart from works is barren? ...You see that a person is justified by works and not by faith alone... For just as the body without the spirit is dead, so faith without works is also dead." (James2:14-21, 24 & 26)

In other words, our faith has to be real and lived out (proven, if you will) — by our works, which are manifestations of our thoughts and our hearts. If we call ourselves Christians, then we need what has been called a "Christian world view," which means that we view all of life, every thought we have and every action we make, through the eyes of Jesus, and through the lens of Scripture. We should never live independently of the Bible, so we must therefore gain its knowledge. We are not to remain in Christian infancy. So, to those who have spent many years claming the title of "Christian," please do not call yourself a Christian (which is a Christ-follower) if you do not know the words, thoughts, and teachings of Christ, if you do not eat them and make them part of yourself. Once you ingest Scripture, you can recover yourself and begin to live out your own call in life. Scripture says, "I urge you to live a life worthy of the call you have received" (Ephesians 4:1). We all do indeed have a call on our lives, which is found in the recovery of ourselves through God's Word and through complete submission to Jesus Christ.

Our Individual Paths

God calls each of us to our own unique paths, and He calls all of us to come out from the world and to be separate from it, since we as Christians are no longer a part of the world's ways, but are to be a "peculiar people" (I Peter 2:9). No one who is a Christ-follower should feel comfortable in this world and within the society that we live. The world is fallen and corrupted by sin, and it should feel foreign and strange to us. God works with each of our unique personalities, as He transforms us, and equips us with the talents and gifts we need to live up to our potential and our calling.

We are not all called into full time ministry, but we are all called to love God through obedience to His Word, the Bible, and to love others unconditionally in whatever setting we live. God is no respecter of persons (Mark 12:14), and He sees us all the same, from the devout nun to the struggling addict. We are called where we are, to love and to obey. In all of our daily lives, we can show the love of Christ as commanded in the Bible in very simple ways. Saint Theresa of Lisieux once said, "Miss no single opportunity of making some small sacrifice, by a smiling look, there by a kindly word; always doing the smallest right and doing it all for love." (Mother Teresa, 75)

I was reminded in a letter from a nun serving at the Missionaries of Charity in Kolkata (formerly Calcutta), India that there are always poor among us. Some people are not financially poor, but there are many who are poor spiritually whom we need to serve right in our own neighborhoods, and we can serve them through our routine, daily lives. Every action we take, every thought we have, must be held captive in Christ Jesus, as we live each moment in the knowledge of the Blueprint so that we do not get lost and confused. "And we take captive every thought to make it obedient to Christ." (II Corinthians 10:5b)

Having great respect and admiration for people such as Mother Teresa, who literally denied herself to follow the call she felt God placed upon her heart, I wanted to go to India to witness first-hand how she and the Missionaries of Charity served the "poorest of the poor." My journey to India caused me to think more seriously about how we are to live out our individual calls, what it truly means to be a Christ-follower, what Scripture commands us to do, what God requires of us, and just what living according to Scripture looks like up close and personal. Each moment of life for the Christian must be lived through the lens of Scripture, which was my focus when I went to India.

Living Our Call
Struggling with the idea of living in and according to Scripture, eating God's word (like Ezekiel did), what it actually means to be a Christ-follower and to live in the fullness of God's will, I decided to take a spiritual pilgrimage to Kolkata (Calcutta), India in order to volunteer at Mother Teresa's Missionaries of Charity. I wanted to begin a spiritual Twelve Step program to enable the process of my own recovery, and I began with a Step One that I called *Develop a Christ-centered world view.*

Mother Teresa had such a tremendous desire to show the love of Jesus to those who were sick, destitute, and dying in a dark, poverty-stricken corner of the world. Through this saintly nun's desire, Mother Teresa found who she was meant to be and how to live completely in God's Word. I want to share some stories from my trip to India that opened the truths of Scripture to me, and I want to explain how the words of the Bible are not merely a segment of our lives, but rather how God's Truth can become our very life. As Paul said in Acts, "For in Him we live, and move, and have our being" (Acts 17:28). Eat the Scriptures. Make the Word of God what you are. Develop a Christ-centered world view, and with each step in life, have Jesus with you while you learn who He is through His Word. The dark streets of India helped bring the truth of my faith (or lack thereof), to light.

Kolkata, India

Before leaving for my trip to India, someone told me that a man who took a mission trip to Kolkata remarked that this city, and specifically the area which houses Mother Teresa's Missionaries of Charity, was the closest thing he could picture to Hell. After traveling to the slums of Kokata myself, I think "Hell" was an accurate description.

I got off of the plane in Kolkata and was hit with hot, dirty, smelly air. It was close to midnight, and I was exhausted after almost thirty hours of flying. Traveling alone, half-way around the world with no one to meet me at the airport, I thought of another step on my spiritual Twelve Step program: *Learn to trust, love, and obey God fully.* I shared a taxi with a fellow, solo American traveler, and we rode almost an hour to my hotel. My new American friend made sure I was safe inside my hotel before he left to go to his hotel, which was on the other side of town. I appreciated this man's concern for my safety and well-being late at night. With each step of my journey, God provided various people to accompany me when I would rather not have been alone. The hotel was clean, and I was brought upstairs to my room, which was small, but had a private bathroom, including a shower! I was thankful, jumped into that shower, basked in the warm, slow trickle of the water, and climbed into a small, clean bed. Little did I know that these few "necessities" would become a source of so much gratitude.

Food and Shelter

In the morning, clean and somewhat refreshed, I went downstairs to the dining area for a wonderful breakfast of two slices of toast, eggs, cooked any way I desired, fresh fruit, coffee or tea, and either cold cereal or porridge. Though it was very generous, this breakfast was nothing out of the ordinary in my every-day life back in America. I can basically eat whatever I have a taste for most days back home. Had I ever before given that luxury much thought? Through the provisions of a fellow traveler who assured my safety, a bed, a toilet, a shower, and now a delicious and plentiful breakfast, in my appreciation, I developed another step in my spiritual recovery: *Learn to see God in daily life.*

After breakfast, I toured Kolkata by taxi, and I found it to be most unpleasant. There were so many people living on the street, including babies and small children literally naked, without even one garment of clothing to wear. I felt ashamed as I thought about the huge suitcase I brought and the large closet full of clothes back home. What about the Scripture that says, "For I was hungry and you gave me no food... naked and you did not clothe me... Truly I tell you, just as you did not do it to one of the least of these, you did not do it to Me" (Matthew 25 — the words of Jesus). I thought to myself, "What is my obligation, and how do I live according to Scripture here in Kolkata?" I began to feel uneasy.

I spent most of the day riding in the taxi and stopping at various sights throughout the city. Kolkata is not much of a tourist trap, and there was not a lot to see, but I hit the highlights. When the driver dropped me off back at the hotel, he told me to give him an outrageous amount of money, according to the going rate of a Kolkata taxi driver. I knew he was trying to cheat this ignorant, "rich" American, and I was angry. I told him to wait, and I would ask at the hotel what I should pay him. I discovered that my driver inflated the price about five times more than the going rate. I paid my driver what the hotel manager and the gate-keeper told me I should pay. The driver was also angry, and I felt nothing. What was happening to me? Why was my heart not breaking from the poverty and desperation of this place, which included my driver? How was Scripture a reality in my life at this point? Was God in my daily life? Honestly, I did not know. Can we move so quickly away from Scripture? Can we move so quickly in the wrong direction? I began to feel lost.

Becoming Invisible

The following day, I went to register as a volunteer at the Missionaries of Charity, which is done on Monday, Wednesday, and Friday at 3:00 p.m. every week. I chose to work at Kalighad, the original site that Mother Teresa began years ago, where the sick and dying homeless people are brought in to be cared for and die among others, on a clean cot, inside a building, rather than alone on a dirty street. Work would begin the following day. It was now dark, and I was unsure where I was (other than a wretched slum), and I needed to get back to my hotel. A rickshaw driver called out to me, so I climbed in the carriage, and off he ran through the dark, narrow streets. The man was dirty, skinny, and haggard; he ran through the slums of Kolkata carrying human cargo just so that he could eat and perhaps provide for a family. I felt a conflict of human rights versus his need to work, with this perhaps being the only work he could do.

When I returned to the hotel, I walked upstairs to a beautiful sitting area; I found a woman I had met the previous night, from Australia, who was also traveling alone, doing PhD research. Here we sat, clean, in this quaint and comfortable room, deciding where we wanted to eat dinner.

The city streets and the rickshaw driver were suddenly a memory as we walked to a restaurant on the "tourist" side of town. Briefly flashing through my mind was the Scripture, "If any want to become My followers, let them deny themselves and take up their cross and follow Me" (Mark 8:34). As quickly as that verse rushed across my mind, it left. How convenient. Where was Scripture at this point in time and how was it the very essence of my life? Honestly, I did not know. Was I eating the words of God, or worried about eating to satisfy my own desires? I began to feel even more lost.

Where Did I Go?

As my new friend and I walked to the restaurant, many street children approached her and were begging for money. We were warned by many people who live in Kolkata, including the Sisters at the Missionaries of Charity, not to give these children anything, as it perpetuates their sad plight. The street children are run by a mafia that takes their money anyway. The evil men of the mafia, who act like pimps to these children, often maim the children so others feel stronger pity for them and give more money. Can evil be any greater than in this brutality? No one can tell me Satan does not exist; he was all around me. The children never approached me for some reason; it was as if I was not there.

Next, a man approached my friend as we continued to walk the streets, and he attempted to strike up a conversation with her. He was one of the many shop-owners who followed and harassed foreigners, as he begged travelers to buy at his shop with the knowledge that most would buy into his highly inflated prices out of ignorance. She politely brushed him off and he walked away. This shop-owner never approached me. I had begun to feel invisible.

We arrived at the restaurant my friend chose, and the waiter greeted my friend and handed her a menu. No one spoke to me. My friend looked at me, and then asked the waiter, "Can you get another menu for my friend?" This repeated scenario of feeling invisible was beginning to get weird. My friend was not being ignored, so I was having difficulty understanding why I became invisible. After dinner, we walked to a café for a cup of tea and dessert, and once again, I was ignored. I was not spoken to by the waiter. I was not handed a menu. I was not asked what I would like. At this point, after discussing this strange, on-going occurrence with my Australian friend, we simply left – without either tea or dessert.

When we returned to the hotel, my friend and I laughed about how I had become invisible that night. I went to my room and contemplated my invisibility. I thought about my hardened heart. I thought about living my life according to Scripture. I realized that if I did not live according to the Bible, I then actually become invisible. Christ, who lives in me, is supposed to be "salt and light," but when I did not reflect that salt and light, by indifference, a hardened heart, or if I did not read Scripture to know who and what I am supposed to be in Christ, then perhaps I would become nothing, as though I were invisible.

> "You are the salt of the earth; but if salt has its taste, how can its saltiness be restored? It is no longer good for anything, but is thrown out and trampled underfoot. You are the light of the world. A city built on a hill cannot be hid. No one after lighting a lamp puts it under the bushel basket, but on the lampstand, and it gives light to all in the house. In the same way, let your light shine before others, so that they may see your good works and give glory to your Father in Heaven" (Matthew 5:13-16).

In failing to be salt and light, in failing to give glory to my Heavenly Father, I became invisible. We are "no longer good for anything" when we are not being salt and light by our failure to be in complete surrender to Jesus and His Word.

I also thought about John the Baptist when he said of himself and Jesus, "He must increase, but I must decrease" (John 3:30). That night, I became invisible. I had been reduced to nothing, which is where I needed to be! I developed another step in my program: *Allow Jesus to be more, and yourself to be less.*

Lost

Wanting to fully experience the sights, sounds, and feel of the crazy, hectic, loud and dirty city of Kolkata, I decided to walk through the streets and get a close up and personal look of dire poverty for myself, and look into the faces and eyes of those who live here in this wretched slum. Many people live on the street, literally; they eat, sleep, bathe, and relieve themselves on the street. The more fortunate ones appeared to live in their shops. In the morning, the shop owners simply rolled up the curtain or opened the doors to begin business for the day. The world is a very small place for the people in the slums of Kolkata. The faces I looked at were faces of desperation, hunger, and emptiness. I looked into their eyes, and saw nothing. In this slum area, I was basically ignored. All of the streets looked the same to me, and as I wound my way through these narrow, dirty, crowded streets, I began to notice how the streets all looked alike, and I began to feel lost. This tiny world, for so many who probably never leave the area, became too large for me, and I realized I had no idea where I was nor how to get back to my hotel. I thought if I just appeared confident and sure, no one would bother me. As I walked and prayed, I believed that God would direct me and keep me safe, which was exactly what happened. We only find our way through Jesus, which I did in prayer as I walked the filthy streets of Kolkata and found my way back to my hotel.

The prophet Jeremiah said, "My people have been lost sheep; their shepherds have led them astray" (Jeremiah 50:6). The prophet Isaiah said, "All we like sheep have gone astray" (Isaiah 53:6). Psalm 119:176 states, "I have gone astray like a lost sheep; seek out your servant, for I do not forget your commandments." How are we found when we are lost? — By obeying, knowing, and seeking out God's commandments through Scripture. How do we even know we are lost unless we first know God's Word, which tells us that we are all quite lost? It was in the filthy streets of India that I began to understand (in more than a theoretical way) that we are all lost and filthy without Jesus; but, by reaching out to Him, He will lead us and guide our paths, no matter where those paths may lead. I developed another step in my spiritual Twelve Step program: *Acknowledge that you are lost.* Until we realize that we are lost, we cannot even begin to move towards recovery.

Pretending
On my first afternoon visiting the "Mother House" (where the nuns live), I met Lisa, a woman about my age who was also traveling alone, and we paired up and became friends for the trip. Again, God provided someone when I needed a friend. It was dark when we decided to leave the Mother House, and we were both unsure how to get back to our respective hotels. A rickshaw driver motioned for me to get a ride with him, so I climbed in. My friend Lisa said she wanted to see the hotel where I was staying since she heard it was the most eccentric hotel in Kolkata (which it was), so she decided to come with me. I told our driver to take us to the hotel on Sudder Street where I was staying, and he nodded and proceeded to go in the wrong direction! I tapped him on his back and said, "The Fairlawn Hotel... You are moving in the wrong direction." He nodded, turned around, and began to jog. I knew we had at least a mile or more to the hotel, but within a few blocks, he stopped and motioned for us to get out. I told him that I would not get out because we were not there yet; he reluctantly continued. I realized our driver did not speak any English and he had no idea where he was going. He stopped a couple of blocks later, again, nowhere near the hotel, and motioned for us to disembark. Once again, we refused, not knowing where we were. I called a woman over who was standing on the street, and I asked if she spoke English; she did, so I asked if she knew where the Fairlawn Hotel was, and if she could relay that information to our driver. She spoke to the driver in their native language, and off he went again. The narrow streets did not look familiar to me, which I told Lisa, and we knew we were lost. Our rickshaw driver took us down a narrow alley, and motioned for us, again, to get out. It was pitch-

black and we had no idea where we were, and so we, again, refused. Our driver began to get angry and we knew he had no idea where he was going; he was only pretending to know. However, like our driver, when we pretend to know something (like the Bible), but really do not have any knowledge, we are placing ourselves and others in danger. Our driver was moving in the wrong direction. I finally saw a building with the words, "Sudder Street," written on it, so we got out, paid him his wage, and headed in the right direction. I thought of my friend's question, "Are we moving in the right direction?" Yes, we can move in the right direction when we have the Blueprint.

I began to think about Scripture and how we need the Truth of that Blueprint every step of the way. We can get so lost with one wrong turn that we begin to fumble through the darkness in fear, unless we know the salt and light of Jesus and how to live out His Word. Unfortunately, many of us think we know where we are going and what we are doing, or we pretend to know, and so we get quite lost along the way. I thought of another spiritual step for my program: *Admit that we all pretend and are hypocritical at times.*

Christianity Versus all other Religions
The following day, I decided to see the famous Hindu Temple called Kalighat, which is also connected to Mother Teresa's Missionaries of Charity, which housed the destitute and dying and where I would be working each day. The taxi-driver could not drive up to the Temple, but he had to park a couple of blocks away; he told me just to walk and I would find it! I was a little confused in the crowds and among the souvenir stands everywhere which sold statues and pictures of gods, along with clothes, toys, etc. Animals and beggars seemed to surround me. People (many crippled) lay on the streets. Women pushed their way towards me with outstretched hands as they looked for me to give them something. Children

squatted to relieve themselves. Animals scrounged through piles of garbage looking for something to eat, as did the destitute. Why such poverty, filth, and hopelessness outside of the Temple? Where was their god?

The Hindu Temple reminded me of the Old Testament description of the Jewish Temple; it was laid out in a courtyard setting with noise and people everywhere. The crowd made it difficult to walk. A man dressed in white escorted me through the Temple area and asked if he could show me around. Since I had no idea where I was, I agreed, though I knew he only appeared kind and helpful so I would pay him. What disturbed me the most was the atmosphere of desperation... desperation to appease their many gods. Prayers were shouted, incense was burned, flowers were tossed into prayer-bowls, and sacrifices were made. I was taken over to a small, enclosed area that still smelled of fresh blood, where goats are sacrificed each day. I was later told at a Methodist church that humans were once sacrificed at this spot, and not all that long ago. I had spoken with other volunteers who saw the head and feet of a goat still in this sacrificial area, and the dogs ran over to grab this fresh meal. I was thankful I did not see the slaughter or its remains; the blood was bad enough!

I was then taken to an area where I was told to remove my shoes, and a string was tied around my wrist almost before I knew what was happening. My "guide" called it a prayer string, and I was told to place the petal of a flower into a bowl, sign a book, and place money in the book that would go to the poor. I realized the "poor" was my guide, and, at this sacred prayer spot, I was being lied to. I thought of a couple of the Ten Commandments as I stood and contemplated what to do (false witness, other gods); I explained that I was a Christian and did not feel comfortable giving money to the Hindu Temple. My guide assured me that my financial gift was alms-giving for the poor, and he suggested that I give a large amount of money. I agreed to give a very small amount, turned, and walked away towards my shoes.

The Temple area was dirty, crowded, loud, and it had a frantic, uneasy feel to me. I felt empty. I sensed an absence of peace and a lack of reverence for God. I felt an absence of love, mercy, and compassion from God. I stood in the midst of noise and a people's frantic desperation to please some god I knew nothing about. There were too many gods within the Temple walls for me to even keep track of. I wanted out. I did not like this place of worship. On my walk out of the Temple, back to the taxi a few blocks away, I thought about my faith, my Jesus, and His incredible love for us. The empty, hollow, desperate eyes of the Hindus in this Temple needed Jesus, and they needed to be embraced by His love and acceptance of them through His blood and the Cross, and not through the blood of goats. The Hindu worshippers at the Temple were frantically searching for some god to accept them while I thought about Jesus Christ, who accepts us just as we are and continually calls us to His love.

Christianity is the only religion where people do not desperately need to earn God's favor (for humans, by their own power, cannot earn His favor). Christianity is the only religion where "God proves his love for us in that while we were still sinners, Christ died for us" (Romans 5:8). Christianity is the only religion where we "earn" God's love and favor simply by acknowledging Him as God and Jesus Christ as the Son of God, who died and rose from the dead to conquer sin and death in our place. All we need to do is accept His amazing gift and love Him back by obeying His Word. We love God by loving others and by living according to Scripture. The Christian faith is quite beautiful, though living the Christian life requires knowing the Bible, the Blueprint, so as not to get lost in a crowded, dirty, frantic and desperate temple of one's own mind. While contemplating the Temple courtyard and the empty faces of the Hindu worshippers, I added another step to my spiritual recovery: *Discover God through Jesus Christ*, Who Himself claimed to be one with the Father God (John 10:30).

Volunteers

The following day I went to the Mother House to begin my volunteer work. I had a rickshaw driver arranged who waited for me at 6:30 a.m. to take me there. My driver did not speak English, other than a few words here and there, but through our smiles and eye contact, we communicated well and became "friends." Down the narrow streets of the wretched slum we went.

We got close to the Mother House, and I told the driver to let me off because I could walk the few, remaining blocks to my destination since we approached a busy street with many taxi drivers (and this traffic did not appear safe for a rickshaw driver). He thanked me, and I walked the loud, crowded street to the Missionaries of Charity. I walked past many people still asleep on the street in the early morning hour, and wondered how they could possibly sleep through all of the city noise.

The Sisters opened the doors for the many volunteers (about fifty), and they fed us a "breakfast" that consisted of a small cup of tea, a tiny banana, and a dry piece of white bread. I complained to myself as I thought about the abundant breakfast at my hotel, which I had paid for and was missing. I immediately felt guilty about my greed, as I thought about my rickshaw driver who slept in his rickshaw outside of my hotel all night, just to take me to this place. I thought about the many homeless people I passed on my walk who would love such a meager breakfast. I was reminded that every moment of my life must be lived in gratitude to Jesus, and that I need to feed continually on the Gospel and to make it a part of my very being. I felt ashamed. I added another step to my Twelve Step program: *Deny yourself for the sake of loving others*. No one said the Twelve Steps would be easy!

Kalighat

Both the city of Kolkata, and Kalighat (the home for the dying), were horrible. The dying, destitute men lived on one side of Kalighat, where the male volunteers worked, and the other side housed the women, where I worked. There were women with leprosy. There were women with tuberculosis. There were women with body lice and with God only knows what other diseases. There were terrified women brought in off the street actively dying. "God," I thought, "How many people die each day out here on the street, and no one knows or cares? How many people die who never heard of you? Who knew nothing of your love and forgiveness, and of Jesus and the Cross?" I began to feel overwhelmed.

One volunteer sat with a tiny, dying, malnourished woman who sat and cried most of the time. I watched this volunteer as she too began to sob, and I walked over and sat down next to her. "This is just too much" she said. "I can't handle this place… these people… it's so awful!"

I put my arm around her, as tears filled my eyes. "I know; it is awful… but you're here with this woman. You are Jesus to her at this moment." She did not understand what I meant. "Come on, let's keep showing these women some love!" We laughed and hugged, and loved. I thought of the Gospels, namely Matthew 25, where Jesus said,

> "Come, you that are blessed by my Father, inherit the kingdom prepared for you from the foundation of the world; for I was hungry and you gave me food, I was thirsty and you gave me something to drink, I was a stranger and you welcomed me, I was naked and you gave me clothing, I was sick and you took care of me, I was in prison and you visited me… Truly I tell you, just as you did it to one of the least of these who are members of my family, you did it to me." (Matthew 25: 34-36 &40)

I was reminded of how grounded in Scripture we need to be in order to live each moment in the very words of God. Each moment in life must be lived for Jesus, and the only way we can be aware of living out our faith is to know what our faith is grounded in and what our faith actually is and requires. Without a solid foundation and knowledge of Scripture, how else can we live as Christians? Some of you may ask, "What difference does it make? Why do I need to know so much Scripture?" Well, here is just one frightening example of what the lack of biblical knowledge can bring, and where such ignorance can lead:

> "'You that are accursed, depart from me into the eternal fire prepared for the devil and his angels; for I was hungry, and you gave me no food, I was thirsty and you gave me nothing to drink, I was a stranger and you did not welcome me, naked and you did not give me clothing, sick and in prison and you did not visit me... Truly I tell you, just as you did not do it to one of the least of these, you did not do it to me.' And these will go away into eternal punishment, but the righteous into eternal life" (Matthew 25:41-43 & 45-46).

For those of us who have a Bible on our shelves (maybe several), ignorance of it will not be an excuse. You may begin to think about dusting it off and reading...

I realized at Kalighat, the other volunteers and I had attempted to live out Jesus' words, as recorded in Matthew 25. I also realized that, right in our own neighborhoods, we could do the same thing, but we usually do not. There are needs everywhere, of all kinds, but in Kolkata, in Kalighat, the needs were enormous, and for some, overwhelming.

Day after day we came to Kalighat to help these dying women. We washed their clothes in big tubs on the floor by hand. We exercised the ladies and tried to help them move, to walk, and we massaged with oil the arms and legs of those women who could not walk. We held their hands. We spoke in languages they could not understand, but they were at least spoken to. We touched them. We fed them and gave them something to drink. We loved them. Through the selflessness of the nuns who lived at the Missionaries of Charity and the long-term volunteers, I thought of another step to my Twelve Step program: *Learn to love and live selflessly.*

Living According to Scripture
I wish I could say I wanted to remain in Kolkata and work at Kalighat, but I cannot. I hated Kolkata with its noise, dirt, poverty, crowds, and the constant begging and deceptions of the poor who lived there. There are many volunteers who remain working in Kolkata for weeks, or months, some even for years! Some of the nuns stay for life! I spent ten days in Kolkata and I wanted to go home after the first week. I longed for my own home, my own bed, food I could actually eat and enjoy, clean air, quiet, solitude, things that were familiar. Part of me wanted to run from the horrors of poverty that were so prominent in this place. I needed to take my own advice.

I came to Kolkata for a spiritual pilgrimage in search of recovery, yet I was feeling more lost than ever. As when I walked through the slums (having been lost), I pretended I knew exactly where I was going. I thought if I just looked like I knew what I was doing and where I was going that no one would know otherwise. Is that what we "Christians" do in life? We go to church on Sunday. We give to the poor. We sing in the choir. We sit on mission boards at church. We carry our Bibles into church, or leave them on the coffee table for all to see while we go through life pretending, looking good, knowing nothing about the faith we profess because we never even read what that faith is?

I wrestled greatly with my struggles in Kolkata, and in my

desire to leave that city. While I did enjoy the work and camaraderie at Kalighat, I enjoyed nothing of India. What if God called me to work in Kolkata full time? Would I tell God no? I felt like I would have to ask Him to go to Plan B. I thought about the words of Jesus: "If any want to become my followers, let them take up their cross daily and follow me" (Luke 9:23). I struggled each day in Kolkata. What if God told me to live here for the rest of my life? Scripture does indeed talk about the disciples leaving everything to follow Jesus. Could I leave everything to serve in Kolkata if God told me to? I did not think I could do that. Paul wrote about dying to himself to live for Christ in Galatians 2:19: " I have been crucified with Christ; it is no longer I who live, but it is Christ who lives in me." If we call ourselves Christians, we are called to live our lives for Christ, not for ourselves and our own desires; we are to love sacrificially and to serve Him. As Christ-followers, we must be willing to go wherever He sends us as the disciples did when they left everything to follow Jesus. Would God call me to Kolkata?

God is not out to make our lives miserable, but God will indeed test our love and commitment to Him at various times in life. He gave us all unique personalities, and He utilizes the desires that He gave us. For example, I love the mountains, and have been interested in eastern Kentucky and the Appalachian culture for many years, even though I am from Chicago. God gave me a job in the heart of Appalachia. However, when the solitude of Appalachia became too great for me, God once again, moved me on. I have always wanted to go to Kenya, and I had a deep passion for Africa. God allowed me to travel to Kenya six times in order to do mission work, and He even threw in a couple of safaris! God knew I had a longing to see Kolkata. I went, though at this point in my life, I do not feel God is calling me to live in Kolkata. God does indeed want to give us the desires of our hearts, and He works in our lives to fulfill our desires as we serve Him, but only if we allow Him and if we are completely surrendered to Him and His will. If the two worlds collide: our hearts desire and our obedience to God through Scripture, we then find recovery of who we were meant to be, and we begin to live in peace; it is a beautiful thing!

Within the struggle of serving the "poorest of the poor" in the slums of Kolkata and my desire to leave the loud and dirty city, I (embarrassingly) discovered another step to my spiritual Twelve Step program: *Understand your will as it conflicts with God's will.* The truth of my own conflict was most apparent.

Ultimate Fulfillment

When we discern God's will in our lives and learn to live in His will, we begin to recover ourselves. Scripture tells us to, "Live a life worthy of your call" (Ephesians 4:1). We must learn to walk in obedience and love if we are to be "worthy," though of course we all fall short of God's perfect standard. The call is never easy; rather, it is filled with trials, temptations, and difficulties, strengthening us and molding us for service, and perhaps even testing us, making us into Kingdom people, the type of people we were created to be. When we read, study, learn and live the Scriptures, and we begin to know and love Jesus and all of humanity, we can then begin recovery and the return to ourselves.

The Center of God's Will

The promises of God, as they are found in Scripture, do not imply that those who know and follow God's Word will at all times have an easy life filled with obvious blessings, and those who ignore God's Word will live lives of obvious pain. Jesus said that His Father in Heaven "makes his sun rise on the evil and on the good, and sends rain on the righteous and on the unrighteous" (Matthew 5:45). We are to live our lives in God's Word because it is the only life that makes sense. Scripture gives us the tools that guide us, that keep us safe, and that will help steer us in the right direction, providing safety and protection while living in God's will.

In discussing his business, Phil Vischer, founder of Veggie Tales, was once asked in a board-meeting where he wanted his new ministry to be in five years. The board members were all prepared to hear this man's insightful business projections, visions and future plans, but they heard something that surprised them instead. Vischer's response was simple: "I want to be in the center of God's will." The Veggie Tale's founder said that he begins each day in prayer and by reading God's Word, which will keep him in that center. We need to begin our days in this same manner. We can only be in God's will when we live according to Scripture and move in the right direction. When we are in the place of surrender, obedience, and love, we can begin to recover who we really are, and who we were meant to be, i.e. we can return to ourselves.

Within the fulfillment of knowing and loving Jesus and His word, I quickly discovered another spiritual step: *Understand safety as found in Scripture and in the center of God's will.*

With a little walking towards Scripture, we are on the road to recovery.

"For to me, living is Christ and dying is gain."
(Philippians 1:21)

CHAPTER SIX

The Wisdom of the Dying

Contemplation
We are given our lifetimes to build solidly and correctly; yet, without the Blueprint, many people build on sand and wonder why, in the end, everything begins to sink and cave in. I began to contemplate my life and my spiritual journey in a much deeper way during my time in India; I reflected on the fact that life is short, and I thought about my spiritual journey thus far in relation to my work as a chaplain. Some people learn to build correctly through the simplicity and joy of life by knowing and following Scripture for many years, while others regretfully learn there was a better way to live while they are literally dying. As a hospice chaplain, I am witness to both situations: lives ending in peace, and lives ending with regrets. Though I am grateful for those people who find Christ on their death beds, I find sorrow in their sad expressions of having wasted their lives, having lived with regrets, and having lost rewards that Jesus promises those who live for Him when they get to eternity. The following pages describe some of the precious people I have had the privilege of meeting personally. Some of my patients' approached the end of their earthly lives having fully understood the beauty of the Scriptures and how they tried their best to live out God's Word. On the other hand, some of my patients' wandered far away from God, only to

learn at the end of their lives that they had been wandering through life lost, sinking in the sand, and without any firm foundation because they did not read their Bibles and therefore did not learn who God is and what He wanted from them. Through the stories of my hospice patients, I continued the journey in my spiritual Twelve Step program of recovery as I listened to many stories in the words of the dying while they contemplated the meaning of their lives in relation to God, love, prosperity, peace, and Truth.

Obedience

"When David's time to die drew near, he charged his son Solomon, saying, 'I am about to go the way of all the earth. Be strong, be courageous, and keep the charge of the Lord your God, walking in his ways and keeping his statutes, his commandments, his ordinances, and his testimonies, as it is written in the Law of Moses, so that you may prosper in all you do and wherever you turn'"(1 Kings 2:1-3). David wanted to pass along the knowledge he gained, the knowledge he understood was important to his son Solomon before he died, since Solomon would be the next king of Israel. David began by telling Solomon to keep the Word of the Law "**so that you may prosper in all you do.**"

God did not give us Scripture to live by in order to tax us with rules to follow that are burdensome. He loves us and wants us to prosper in everything we do, which is promised over and over throughout Scripture. Prosperity does not imply that we will not face hardships, pain, and difficulties in life, but it does mean we are always in the safety, plan, and purpose of God's will. When we walk closely with God and His Word, even in the slums of Kolkata, we can prosper. Prosperity involves a life of inner peace, security, and love in Christ, which comes through a life submitted to Jesus and His Word. Don't we all want to recovery in prosperity?

Step One

In my own journey through India and with the dying in hospice, I realized that, during much of my life, I did not live as a Christ-follower, yet I called myself a Christian. I painfully realized the first step of my spiritual Twelve Step journey: *Admit that we all pretend and are hypocritical at times.*

The Bible often repeats the theme of submission to God, not *asking* us, but *commanding* us to obey Him for our own good. King David knew this truth as he was dying, and, in some of his last words to his son, he reminded Solomon of this truth. I too have heard from the mouths of dying people the importance of understanding Jesus and keeping the Word of God for our own good — and their words were very powerful.

Step Two

There is a powerful truth that I heard a dying man say to me, though rarely have I heard it from or seen evidence of it in those who are very much alive; this truth is found in Proverbs 1:7 which says, "The fear of the Lord is the beginning of knowledge." If the fear of God is only the **beginning,** then all else certainly follows. To live in the fear of God means that we realize He has all of life and death in His hands, and we honor, revere, and worship Him, as our relationship of love grows each day for Him. The fear of the Lord is a healthy reverence and respect for the Creator of the Universe. How many of us actually live our lives in the fear of the Lord? If we did, we would not take His Word, His commands, and our sins so lightly.

As a chaplain in rural Appalachia, I drove out to what seemed like the middle of nowhere, down a narrow "holler" in the mountains, to the run-down home of Arnold, a dying man. Arnold lived with his wife, and, at the time of my visit, his brother was visiting, who played his banjo and sang for this lovely couple. We engaged in small-talk for a while, and we all enjoyed listening to the banjo music and had fun singing, "I'll Fly Away" several times. I then asked Arnold and his wife if they would like to take the Lord's Supper the following week, Holy week, since they could no longer get to church, and would miss Good Friday and Easter services. His wife was thrilled and said that she would like to have communion, but her husband Arnold (the patient) said something that surprised me. He said in a weak voice from his bed, "I don't know; I don't want to eat and drink condemnation to myself. I've fallen away from the Lord and haven't even been to church in years." I asked Arnold why he said that, though I knew he was referring to Scripture; he said, "It's in the Bible!"

Paul was explaining to the Corinthian church about the Lord's Supper in 1 Corinthians 11:27-32:

> "Whoever, therefore, eats the bread or drinks the cup of the Lord in an unworthy manner will be answerable for the body and blood of the Lord. Examine yourselves, and only then eat of the bread and drink of the cup. For all who eat and drink without discerning the body, eat and drink judgment against themselves. For this reason many of you are weak and ill, and some have died. But if we judged ourselves, we would not be judged. But when we are judged by the Lord, we are disciplined so that we may not be condemned along with the world."

My patient, knowing he was dying of cancer, knew enough of the Bible to have a fear of the Lord. Arnold knew what the Lord's Supper represented: the agonizing torture and death of Jesus when He was crucified on the cross for the forgiveness of our sins. Jesus willingly took our place by momentarily experiencing the separation from God that we all deserve forever, but will not have to endure if we love and trust Jesus Christ. Arnold knew he grew away from his Savior and did not follow Jesus as he once had and became lost along the way, which brought me to the next step in my spiritual recovery: *Acknowledge that you are lost.* In humility, Arnold acknowledged his lost, regretful state.

How often have any of us taken the Lord's Supper, knowing we were living in some unrepentant sin, but did so out of habit or fear of what others in the church might have thought if we did not partake? Has this warning in Scripture from 1 Corinthians ever passed though your mind in church if you have ever been in a sinful situation, yet continued to live in it and still took part in the Lord's Table? Have you ever failed to examine yourself prior to communion? Do we really take Scripture seriously? Do we really fear God? Solomon, the writer of Ecclesiastes knew the fear of the Lord when he wrote, "Though sinners do evil a hundred times and prolong their lives, yet I know that it will be well with those who fear God, because they stand in fear before him, but it will not be well with the wicked, neither will they prolong their days like a shadow because they do not stand in fear before God" (Ecclesiastes 8:12-13). How would we even know to fear God and take the Lord's Supper so seriously? — By knowing Jesus and by reading the Bible.

Step Three
Even though I was warned, I was unprepared for what I saw. Dan was retaining fluid in his head for some reason, which even the doctors could not quite understand. I had seen Dan a couple of weeks prior to this particular visit, and other than the fact that he was dying, he was physically "normal." However, something drastic happened to Dan since my last visit. Dan's head was about twice its normal size, and his eyes were swollen shut, with the lids and surrounding skin about the size of golf balls. His lips were swollen and spread over his nose. He was a small, slight man who was quite thin, which seemed to exaggerate the swollen head and made it appear huge. Dan did not appear human. Of course, as the chaplain (and as a human being), I had to pretend that I was

not shocked by the sight of Dan. However, I was not only shocked, but repulsed with sadness and pity for this poor man. His girlfriend sat on the hospital bed with him, held his hand, and said, "Guess what? Dan is going to be baptized Sunday!"

"Oh my goodness, I am so excited!" I exclaimed.

Dan told me on my first visit to him that he wanted to "get his life together" before he died. Dan had seven children by four different women. His terminal illness was the result of thirty years of heavy drinking, smoking, and self abuse. He had begun going to church a couple of months ago, and the pastor had shown him in Scripture where Peter said, "Repent, and be baptized every one of you in the name of Jesus Christ so that your sins may be forgiven; and you will receive the gift of the Holy Spirit" (Acts 2:38). In Eastern Kentucky, if you are going to get baptized (especially in the Old Regular Baptist Church), you go to the creek and are submerged; that is the only way a baptism is done there.

Dan had a few medical conditions that needed to be discussed with his nurse. First of all, Dan had a feeding tube extending out of his stomach and a trachea tube in his throat, so with both of these areas being exposed and open, infection was, of course, a concern in a muddy creek. The pastor and nurse discussed these potentially dangerous issues, and decided that gauze bandages, towels and other precautions could be taken, in addition to a very quick dunk! Dan was also very weak and needed assistance walking, so his son would help get him into the creek. In my (I admit, vain) mind, I wondered if Dan was not at all self-conscious about his appearance? Be that as it may, Dan said the Bible instructs us to believe and to be baptized, so that was what he was going to do.

For some people, Dan's baptism might have appeared to be too much trouble. There were too many precautions to be taken, and a thirty minute car-ride to the creek is a lot to go through for a dying man. Dying people are weak, sick, tired, and generally do not take long car rides for any reason, but Dan was determined to follow Scripture, especially when he knew his time here on Earth was drawing to a close. As his girlfriend was telling me about the baptism, Dan held my hand tightly. He could not talk since his lips, tongue, and throat were too swollen for him to speak. He could not look at me, since his eyes were swollen shut, so I was not sure what he was thinking or feeling; but, he appeared to be smiling at me as he held and rubbed my hand tightly. I think Dan was trying to communicate to me that we would probably never see one another on this earth again, and he wanted me to know that he was obediently following Scripture and trusting in Jesus his Savior for his eternity.

Dan's obedience was remarkable, despite all of the "mountains" in his life and his impending death. Why do so many of us wait until our bodies are racked with disease until we realize the need to follow Scripture? Had he lived his life according to the Blueprint God so graciously laid out for us, Dan might not have experienced the situation that he was in. God's grace is so amazing, isn't it? Despite Dan's life of disobedience, in his final weeks, God still heard His child's voice. God loves us, forgives us, and reaches down and saves all who come to Him. Dan finally understood. Dan discovered a truth that is included in my spiritual Twelve Steps: *Discover God through Jesus Christ*. He was indeed baptized, and he died shortly after his obedient response to Scripture. At the funeral home, the pictures of Dan's baptism surrounded his coffin. How did Dan know he was to believe and to be baptized, and would receive forgiveness? — By knowing Jesus through reading the Bible.

Step Four

"For if you forgive others their trespasses, your heavenly Father will also forgive you; but if you do not forgive others, neither will your Father forgive your trespasses" (Matthew 6:14-15). I never met two people who exemplified the concept of forgiveness more than Ken and Pat. However, neither have I heard of such an extreme need to forgive as well!

I parked at the top of a steep, winding, gravel hill and walked several "blocks" down to the tiny old wooden house where my patient and his family lived. I laughed at the old toilets outside that now served as flower pots, and I watched the chickens, dogs, and cats run around the yard, past the cars that sat up on blocks, perhaps reminding the family of trips taken in the past. I knocked on the wooden door and heard someone tell me to come on in. I walked into a tiny living room where my patient lay in a hospital bed, surrounded by his attentive family. With no air-conditioning on this hot summer day, the room was sweltering and stuffy, though I pretended to be comfortable.

Pat was trying to lift a blanket to cover her dying husband, but she was having some difficulty. I noticed all of the fingers on her left hand were gone except for her thumb and pinkie. I could not help but look, which she noticed. "It's hard sometimes with this hand. I got all of my fingers blown off with a shot gun," she said in such a matter-of-fact manner.

"What?!" I asked with surprise.

She replied, "Oh, his father (pointing to her husband, our hospice patient who was sitting up in his bed) shot at us with a shot gun. I put my hand up to protect my husband and tried to get the door closed, and my fingers got blown away. He got hit in the neck — see the scar?" She pointed to the scar on his neck. I could hardly believe what I was hearing!

"Tell me about this, Pat" I said.

"Well, he just came after us with a shot gun, that's all," and she spoke as if this were a normal event!

I asked the obvious question, "Why?!"

"Oh, because his wife told him to; she said, 'Shoot that SOB!' He was afraid of his wife, so he did whatever she told him. She was mean."

I then asked, "She said that about her own son? Her birth son?"

"Yes," she replied. I was dumbfounded, but Pat relayed this story as if it were a daily event. Ken said nothing.

"What happened after that? Did they come after you guys again? Were you afraid? Did you go to the police?" I was filled with questions!

"No. They never came after us again. I was sure they wouldn't. He came to us later and asked for our forgiveness."
I then asked, "Did you forgive him?"

She did not hesitate for a moment, "Of course! I asked if he asked the Lord for forgiveness, and he said he did, so if God could forgive him, then I must too."

"Did your husband forgive his dad?"

"Yes."

I then inquired, "What about his mother, the one who told her husband to shoot at you both?"

"Oh, she never asked us for forgiveness, but we forgave her. We actually didn't even see her until she was dying. I held her hand as she died."

I was amazed. I was amazed, first of all, with this story (which seemed incomprehensible to me); but, even more so, I was amazed at the forgiveness that was so freely offered. She made it sound so simple. Pat had long lived out one of the steps that was reinforced on my journey: *Begin to develop a Christ-centered world view.* The Bible says to forgive... so you forgive! How did she know we are commanded to love and to forgive? — By knowing Jesus and by reading the Bible.

Step Five

Larry was dying of Parkinson's disease. He was totally bed-bound, and he could not move much of his body at all. When his third wife discovered he was dying, she left him. Larry was, of course, very angry, and his anger was compounded by the fact that his two sons (by other wives) rarely saw him. Larry called to inform his sons that he was dying. Apparently, there was a lot of former, relational damage in his family, and his sons remained estranged from him. Larry's wife left him, his sons abandoned him, and his body failed him. Fortunately, Larry's sister, Sandy, took him in to her home to live out his remaining days. Sandy lived in an old, small, single-wide trailer in the middle of a yard of mud. There were no grassy areas, no flowers, and no trees around the trailer, but the only thing surrounding the home, for what felt like miles, was mud. Larry's life consisted of lying in bed, looking out of the large picture-window in the living room onto a "field" of mud and having his sister take care of him. Sandy's friend, Randy, hung a hummingbird feeder outside on the front porch in Larry's field of vision to give him something beautiful to view during his long days. Sandy spent her days taking care of her brother Larry and her nights sleeping on the couch next to him in order to assist him as needed.

One day, Sandy, Larry's sister, was frying some potatoes, and a grease-fire exploded. Because they lived in a trailer, the fire quickly spread and the trailer began to melt. Larry had his oxygen on, since he could not breathe well, which should have exploded, but it did not. Sandy, and her friend who was visiting at the time, quickly fled the house, called the fire department, and tried to get back in to rescue Larry, who could not move. Larry called out to his panicked sister, but the heat and flames prevented her from reaching him. Flames engulfed his room. When the fire department arrived, they told Sandy and her friend, who were now both outside, that there was no way they could reach her brother, and with the thick, black smoke and the quickly spreading fire, he must be dead by now anyway. Sandy's friend could not accept this statement from the fireman, and she broke a window in the back bedroom where Larry helplessly lay, despite warnings not to do so by the fire department. In the horror of the flame-engulfed room, Sandy's friend pulled the catheter out of Larry, tore the oxygen mask off of his face, and dragged him through the broken window. Despite the fact that the hospital bed was melted, the television completely burned, as well as was everything else in Larry's bedroom, he was totally unharmed, without a scratch, bruise, burn, or singe on his body!

As the family was recounting this story to me, I asked Larry if he was in a panic at the time of the fire. Larry calmly said, "No. I heard a voice tell me that I would be alright, and then I felt a hand surround me and protect me from the flames. I knew it was God." Larry said he was not a believer, though he was an avid reader and had read the Bible. He rarely went to church, he was "mean, a woman chaser, and a wild sinner," but through this experience, he knew God was giving him one last chance of salvation. He knew he was dying of a disease, and he was thankful God spared him from the fire in order to come to Jesus before he died. Larry calmly saw God in the midst of disaster, and he caused me to think of another spiritual step: *Learn to see God in daily life.* Larry said he was now calm, he was no longer angry, and he said that he was "a new person since Jesus came into [his] life." Larry understood grace. I understood grace in a whole new way, and I realized just how much safety there is in God's grace. How did Larry and I know that God is so full of grace, love, and mercy? — By knowing Jesus and by reading the Bible.

Step Six

As a hospice chaplain, I am often privileged to experience the best in people. Caregivers of the dying pull from reserves they never thought they possessed, as caring for a dying loved one is probably the most difficult task a person can perform in this life. God gives strength and wisdom when the well begins to run dry, and these new and painful challenges are met head on and are done almost without thinking. God is at work. God is visible through these people, for God is love.

I drove into a deep, Appalachian "holler," through some of the most beautiful country I have seen, to visit Ann, the primary care giver/daughter of a patient who died the previous day. I wanted to see how she was emotionally and spiritually handling the death of her mother whom she loved dearly. Ann was a large, strong woman of my same age, and she met me on the porch with a big hug and a smile. She pulled up two white rocking chairs on the large front porch and asked me to sit down. In the usual, southern hospitality, Ann went to the kitchen and came back with two glasses of iced tea for us to drink. As we sat and rocked, we listened to the creek waters cascade over the rocks and we looked out at the beauty of the mountains. The horses watched us for a while, and then they ate some grass, as if life remained the same each day. Silently, we watched the beauty of these strong, graceful animals, and I almost envied the freedom the horses appeared to live in as they ran through the tall grass with seemingly no cares or concerns or sadness.

Ann began to talk about her mom and how difficult it was taking care of her as she watched her slowly die; but, she said she did so with no regrets. Living without regrets, I feel, is important. What was intriguing about listening to Ann talk was her humility and her strength. She said to me, "I had no idea what I was doing half the time, taking care of mom. People asked me how I did it, and I said 'I don't know, you just do what you do!' Remember I used to tell you when you came to visit that I didn't know what to do sometimes? But God gives you what you need when you need it. He's got it goin' on! He's an awesome God!" Ann lovingly denied herself to take care of her mother. I saw her live out a step in my Twelve Step journey: *Deny yourself for the sake of loving others.* How did she know God gives us the resources we need? — By knowing Jesus and by reading the Bible.

Step Seven
Ann's mom Clara was an amazing woman. I loved to visit Clara and her daughter, Ann. They lived together in an old home, on more acres than I could see, at the end of a long, dirt road. Their home was tucked into the Appalachian Mountains and was built on a large, green field surrounded by horses and vegetable gardens. Creeks ran through their property, and the sound of the running waters over the rocks was always soothing and beautiful. The old farm-house was large, well-kept, and very comfortable. Ann and Clara were very good hostesses, and, each time I came to visit, they both made me feel very welcomed, and they offered me a cup of coffee or iced tea. Both mother and daughter were quite polite and kind, and they were also very humble.

I often told Clara that I admired her faith and strength and that I enjoyed visiting her. Clara suffered with oral cancer and was often in great pain; she would hold a damp washcloth to her swollen face most of the day. One particular day, I asked Clara about her pain and how she was dealing with it. Clara said, "It's ok. I will never suffer as Jesus did for us when He hung on the cross, so I can't complain." I was dumbfounded, and I told her how much I respected her for her faith and her courage. She just shrugged and smiled at me, as if her comment was merely a statement of fact, which it was for her (but not for most people). I also commented with each visit how considerate she was to me, since she always asked if I wanted coffee or anything to eat or drink, if I had enough light, if I was comfortable where I was sitting, and how I was doing that day. There she was, in pain while she suffered and was literally dying... yet, she was always concerned for me, a stranger, as well as any other person who was with her, and, of course, for her daughter who tended to her every need day and night. Most healthy people are not that considerate on a daily basis! Clara consistently lived out one of my Twelve Steps: *Allow Jesus to be more, and yourself to be less.* How did she know such sacrificial love? — By knowing Jesus and by reading the Bible.

Step Eight
I had visited with Ivan for several months on a weekly basis. Ivan lived about five miles into a deep, narrow "holler" in a tiny, wooden house with one of his sons. The house was usually dirty, but Ivan's daughter and neighbor came about once a week to clean. Ivan was bed-bound, so his hospital bed was next to a large picture window in the living room that looked out onto the mountains. Ivan was often depressed with his inability to walk or do anything more in life than to look out the window, watch the birds and the leaves blow in the wind, and listen to the ticking of the clock on the wall.

When I first met Ivan, he was a crabby, unhappy man, angry with his physical limitations, his boredom, his cramped legs, and his inability to get out of bed. Ivan did not want anyone to "bother" him. In gentleness, I persisted, and I finally broke through. Ivan began to look forward to my visits, which I grew to enjoy! Ivan was 92 years old, and he was baptized in a creek at the age of 89 — in his wheelchair! On one of my visits, Ivan said to me, "I heard a voice... I think it was the Lord, who told me that if I were to get baptized I would walk again. Well, you saw those pictures; I got baptized, and I haven't walked since! I guess maybe it wasn't the Lord after all, since He doesn't lie... but I was sure that it was."

I looked at Ivan for a minute, and said, "Maybe it was the Lord, and maybe He meant that you will indeed walk again, but in Heaven."

Ivan began to cry. "I have a lot of dreams you know," Ivan said. "I had a dream that I was walking all over this house, and then I began to walk in the clouds. Maybe you're right. I know there's a place in the Bible that talks about the new bodies we'll get." I walked over and got his huge, large-print Bible that he had received at his baptism, and turned to 1 Corinthians 15. I read most of the chapter, but emphasized the verses beginning at verse 50-57:

> "Flesh and blood cannot inherit the kingdom of God, nor does the perishable inherit the imperishable. Listen, I will tell you a mystery! We will not all die, but we will all be changed, in a moment, in the twinkling of an eye, at the last trumpet. For the trumpet will sound, and the dead will be raised imperishable, and we will all be changed. For this perishable body must put on imperishability, and this mortal body must put on immortality. When this perishable body puts on imperishability, then the saying that is written will be fulfilled: 'Death has been swallowed up in victory. Where, O death, is your victory? Where, O death, is your sting?' The sting of death is sin, and the power of sin is the law. But thanks be to God, who gives us victory through Jesus Christ our Lord."

Ivan looked into my eyes and said, "Oh, I wish all people would be saved. I want them all to have new bodies, and for none to perish... but I know we must believe and follow Christ for our eternity. I just wish all knew Him, and I believe in every word of that Bible."

"I wish that were so, Ivan. I wish that were so," I replied.

Ivan truly loves all people. He lived out another step in my journey: *Learn to love, help and live selflessly.*

How was Ivan able to discern God's voice and develop such a love for all people? — By knowing Jesus and by reading the Bible.

Step Nine
Bob was in a lot of pain as he suffered terribly from bone cancer. Shortly after my visit to him and his wife in their home, he was taken away by ambulance in a pain-crisis. Bob had been a pastor for twenty years, and, through his suffering, he had never doubted or questioned God. Years ago, their oldest son died in a car accident. Shortly after this tragedy, Bob was not feeling well, and he thought perhaps he was suffering from grief, as he and his wife struggled in their pain. Neither Bob nor his wife ever lost their faith in Jesus, and they always knew that God is a good God who loves us. Bob's wife, Christy, said their son died with a smile on his face and was clutching his Bible. The rescue workers believed he had a heart attack before he crashed, and when they arrived at the scene, they said they were all brought to their knees in tears and prayer. Christy, through her tears, said if her son had to die for others to be led to the Lord, then good came out of it. Christy knew their son would be at peace and that he was face-to-face with Jesus now.

At the time of their son's death, Bob continued to feel worse with each day. Bob had gone to a doctor, who was also a friend of his, who told him nothing was wrong with him. The doctor said that Bob was merely suffering from grief and from the pain that resulted from a previous mining accident, where Bob was crushed and nearly died. Time went by, and Bob got worse. He again went to his doctor friend and Bob and Christy asked if he could see a specialist. The doctor never gave the referral, even after several attempts for him to do so. A year later, Bob was pretty sick, and he finally got a referral since his pain was quickly increasing. It was discovered that Bob had stage-four bone cancer, and he was declared terminal.

Bob said that his other son asked him one day how he would know if he was really a Christian or not. Bob gave a very simple, yet profound, answer. He said, "You know you are a Christian and are following Jesus when your greatest desire is to follow His will, despite your own desires, and that you love others more than yourself. That's how you know." Bob explained to his son another step of my journey: *Understand your will as it conflicts with God's will.* Despite Bob's diagnosis, he continued to follow these commands, and he even loved the doctor friend who misdiagnosed him and may have cost him his life.

Bob knew Jesus and Scripture, and he lived in the Truth of God's Word. Bob knew that Jesus said to His disciples, "If any want to become my followers, let them deny themselves and take up their cross and follow me" (Matthew 16:24). He also knew Paul wrote, "Do nothing from selfish ambition or conceit, but in humility regard others as better than yourselves" (Philippians 2:3). Scripture also speaks of loving others more times than I can even begin to list, and most Christians are familiar with "the love chapter" of 1 Corinthians 13, which defines love. How did Bob develop such a passion for Jesus and for others? — By knowing Jesus and by reading the Bible.

Step Ten

I was at the home of another patient, Rose, an elderly woman who was a wonderful, tender lady of God and had been a Christian for over sixty years. Rose appreciated her chaplain visit each week because she told me that she loved having someone to talk to about the Lord who was excited about the Lord, who wanted to pray with her and to hear her thoughts about her Savior. It was a delight to visit this woman. Rose lived in a comfortable home with her husband of about 60 years. Rose's son, Tom, stayed with his parents most of the time to help out, despite having a wonderful family of his own; he was a warm, funny, Christian man who, with tears in his eyes, often spoke tenderly about his mother. Tom sometimes sat in Rose's bedroom with her and me and spoke about what a wonderful example his mother was of a fine, strong, Christian woman whom everyone loved, including him. Cards, pictures, flowers and gifts in the bedroom displayed the love and affection many people had for Rose. Her warmth, tenderness, and love were apparent, even while she lay dying with an oxygen mask, often struggling to breathe. Rose could not get out of bed, so her family planted a beautiful flower-garden outside her window and hung bird-feeders for her so that she could watch the birds come and go. Wind-chimes sang in the breeze while the birds seemed almost to dance to the melody.

On one of my visits, Rose was talking about her approaching death, and she admitted that, sometimes, she was a little afraid. I asked her why she was scared, since she knew Jesus and was assured of her salvation. She looked straight into my eyes, with tears, and said, "I am so sinful, and I know Jesus forgives me, but I wonder what I will feel like when I see Him. We all fall so far short." While she knew Jesus died on the cross for our forgiveness and bore our sins so that we can have eternal life and be with Him in Paradise, she also knew she was close to being in Paradise, face-to-face with God.

She began to see the holiness of God. My patient, however, trusted God for her salvation, which was another step in my program: *Learn to trust, love, and obey God completely.*

In Leviticus 11:44 & 45, God said, "Be holy, for I am holy." Peter also reminded us of the truth of God's holiness in 1 Peter: "...discipline yourselves; set all your hope on the grace that Jesus Christ will bring you when he is revealed. Like obedient children, do not be conformed to the desires that you formerly had in ignorance. Instead, as he who called you is holy, be holy yourselves in all your conduct; for it is written, 'You shall ***be holy, for I am holy***'" (emboldened italics mine). How did this woman know of God's holiness, and her sinfulness and yet still be able to die in peace? — By knowing Jesus and by reading the Bible.

Step Eleven
Maude knew the power of Scripture, the grace of God, and the strength her old, sick body could find in Christ as she fought the battle of sin, apathy, ignorance and the lukewarm nature of many "Christians." Maude had submitted her will to God long ago, though Maude's family did not understand her spiritual battle and subsequent spiritual recovery. However, it was in her own journey and struggle that Maude found recovery in Christ, and she prospered in the midst of her physical poverty in rural Appalachia.

The directions to Maude's home led me to a house that I thought no one could possibly live in. The house, or rather, the run-down shack was on a hill that I could not even force my car to ascend; so, I parked at the bottom of the gravel driveway and walked up to the old house. Dogs, cats, and chickens greeted me on my ascent, and they appeared to be almost dying for love and attention. A woman shouted down to me from the front porch (that I was sure would collapse under her weight, though she seemed unaffected by the disrepair),

"You must be the hospice nurse?"

"No," I said. "Hope I don't disappoint you, but I'm the chaplain." We both laughed. "Can I come in?" I asked.

"Sure. Come on through the gate," which almost fell down when I gently opened it. As I walked toward the house, I heard a tap on a window, and I saw an old woman sitting, looking out, and she motioned for me to come in. I walked around to the back of the house to a porch with a ceiling that was barley six feet high, and I opened the old, broken-down door to the kitchen where Maude sat. It was a warm, June afternoon, but she sat in front of an open oven door wrapped in a blanket, and she wore a flannel night-shirt and pajamas. She reached out to me and as I hugged her, she cried, "Oh thank you Jesus for sending me this woman." I do not think she even knew who I was! "Get yourself a chair and sit with me," she said. I went into the next room, got an old wooden chair, sat close to her, and held her hand as she started to speak. "I just want someone to hear me, to listen to my dreams, to hear my stories."

"That's what I'm here for," I said.

Maude said, "Everyone is so busy, they don't have time to sit and listen, and they think I'm crazy. I just want someone to fight with me in this battle. Do you have time?"

"Yes, I have time to listen," I said. "Tell me your dreams, and tell me about this battle." The "battle" that Maude discussed was the battle waged between good and evil, righteousness and sin. It was very apparent that, even in the last stages of her life, Maude was very concerned about living according to Scripture.

Maude proceeded to tell me dreams about her long-ago

deceased father, in vivid detail, and then, with tears in her eyes, she said, "Who will fight this battle with me? There is just so much sin in the world, and no one cares. Will you fight with me?"

I looked intently into her eyes and said, "Yes, Maude; I will fight this battle with you because you are right. There is so much sin in this world." I thought of a verse in II Chronicles 20:15 that says, "Thus says the Lord to you: 'Do not fear or be dismayed at this great multitude; for the battle is not yours but God's.'" Maude was sick and tired of all the sin and corruption in the world and the lack of love among people. Maude said she wanted to fight the evils and sins of this world and stand against the lukewarm faith of the Church. Maude said that she was hurt by the indifference people felt towards Scripture and Jesus. I was in full agreement. I also thought of Ephesians 6:10-17:

> "Finally, be strong in the Lord and in the strength of his power. Put on the whole armor of God, so that you may be able to stand against the wiles of the devil. For our struggle is not against enemies of blood and flesh, but against the rulers, against the authorities, against the cosmic powers of this present darkness, against the spiritual forces of evil in heavenly places. Therefore take up the whole armor of God, so that you may be able to withstand on that evil day, and having done everything, to stand firm. Stand therefore, and fasten the belt of truth around your waist, and put on the breastplate of righteousness. As shoes for your feet put on whatever will make you ready to proclaim the gospel of peace. With all of these, take the shield of faith, with which you will be able to quench all the flaming arrows of the evil one. Take the helmet of salvation, and the sword of the Spirit, **_which is the word of God_**" (emboldening, italics, and underlining are mine).

The Word of God, the Bible, is our greatest weapon in this battle against the lukewarm love and apathy of much of the Church. The Word of God is what Jesus used against Satan when He was tested by him in the wilderness. If Jesus Christ needed Scripture in His battle against the enemy, how much more do we? Maude was aware of a battle, because it is in the Bible. I prayed with Maude, and, together, we remembered whose battle it really is. The battle belongs to the Lord, but we are still on the battlefield, and we can still recover. I thought about a step in my spiritual Twelve Step program as I listened to Maude: *Understand safety as found in Scripture and in the center of God's will.* We can only find safety on the battlefield through God. How do we know about the battle of sin, apathy, ignorance and a lack of love and submission? — By knowing Jesus and by reading the Bible.

Step Twelve
George touched my soul like few others have in my life. He was dying of cancer, and he knew and loved the Lord with all his heart, though for much of his life he did not. While lying in bed dying, George shared the Lord with everyone who came into his room: nurses, doctors, friends, family... anyone and everyone. George loved people, and would ask me when I came to see him to write down the names of his friends who were not Christian so that my church would pray for them. George wanted everyone he knew to be saved and to live for Jesus. Despite the fact that he was dying, George was one of the most considerate people I have ever known.

A couple of months before his death, I told George that I was taking a short mission trip to India, so he gave me a book to read on the plane (which I loved and highly recommend — *A Hole in the Gospel,* by Richard Stearns). He was always thinking of others and what he could do for people. Two days before George died he told me how he had led a friend of his to the Lord from his hospital bed. George simply wanted others to know Christ. Each time I would tell George how much I loved and respected him for his heart of love for Jesus and others, he would say, "Well I know works won't get me to Heaven, but I have a lot of missed time to make up for." George had a lot of regrets for a life not lived for the Lord, other than the last several years. The closer George came to the end of his earthly life, the more he seemed to love Jesus. He never became angry or bitter, even though he was leaving a 15-year-old son, whose mother had died 12 years earlier. George went ahead and made all of the necessary plans he needed, and he just loved Jesus and others. Many times when I would come to visit, George would be listening to the Bible on CD. He learned to love God's Word, and it changed George dramatically. George, through the power of the Holy Spirit and the Word of God, really learned to love, which is what Scripture teaches; it changes hearts and minds.

The day before George died, I walked into his room; he looked at me, closed his eyes, and said, "Donna, it's just about that time." I asked George if he was scared, and he said that he was not. I asked if he felt peace, and he said that he did (with a smile). "I'm tired" he said. He was ready. I stayed with George for about an hour or so, but I had other patients to see that day as well. George asked if I would see him the next day, and I told him that I would try. God is good. I was supposed to go to a meeting about 45 minutes away, and I would then be going in the opposite direction to see other patients, but the location of the meeting was changed suddenly to our office, right across the street from the hospital where George was staying. I went to see him after the meeting, and he looked bad. George was drowning in fluid, and was having difficulty breathing. He began to panic a little and said he was being smothered and that he could not catch his breath. He began reciting Psalm 23. "Say it with me!" George said, as he grabbed my arm. Together, we began saying this beautiful Psalm, as I hit the nurses' call button. I then held George and we prayed together. Within minutes, the nurse came into the room, and I asked her to help him with his breathing and anxiety, and a short time later, George was given a shot that helped with both. George relaxed as I held his hand, and I asked if he wanted me to read Scripture to him. George smiled and nodded positively since he was too weak to talk. I read page after page to him, and he smiled. George wanted to hear Scripture as he left this earth to be in the presence of Jesus. George fell asleep, and a couple of hours later, he woke up in Heaven. While literally dying, George knew the power of Scripture, the power of Jesus' love, and the love of other Christians. George knew the power of God's love, expressed through His Word. God is love. George quietly left this earth, and he recovered through Scripture and its power to change minds, to change hearts, and to change lives. George lived and died in the love of Jesus and in the power of Scripture, which I am still learning in my spiritual recovery: *Recover yourself through Scripture.*

Recovery
The stories I have recounted of these dying people display God's love, grace, mercy, and desire for us all to find recovery through Him. Through His Word, God places a path before us, but many have chosen, for one reason or another, to ignore the Blueprint. God's love is so relentless that, even while we lay on a death-bed, He still speaks to us and affirms His love for us. God was there for people who already knew Him and found recovery through Him. God is also there for those, like Larry, who formerly had ignored Him... and by this ever-present grace of God, Larry found recovery as he lay dying. God never gives up on us. My heart longs to find *complete* recovery of who I was meant to be while I am still healthy, and I desire to walk *completely* in the call God placed on my life while I still have life within me. The safest place to be is in the center of God's will and in His grace.

Obedience and a love for Scripture will allow you to find your way back to Jesus, to a deep love for God and for others, and to recover yourself as He meant for you to be.

> **"The end of the matter; all has been heard: Fear God, and keep his commandments; for that is the whole duty of everyone. For God will bring every deed into judgment, including every secret thing, whether good or evil."**
>
> **(Ecclesiastes 12:13-14)**

"Very truly, I tell you, unless a grain of wheat falls into the earth and dies, it remains just a single grain; but if it dies, it bears much fruit. Those who love their life will lose it, and those who hate their life in this world will keep it for eternal life. Whoever serves me must follow me, and where I am, there will my servant be also. Whoever serves me, the Father will honor."
(John 12:24-26)

CONCLUSION

The Process of Recovery

The Radical Words of Jesus
The words on the preceeding page are the words of Jesus, shortly before He was betrayed by His friend and disciple Judas, tortured, and put to death on a cross. Jesus said that those who serve Him must follow Him and will be where He is. We like to think that Jesus is referring to Heaven, but what is the context of this verse in the Gospel of John? Jesus was about to die! He mentioned a grain of wheat dying in order to bring forth fruit or life. Jesus is telling us that we must die to this world and to ourselves, like the grain of wheat, and we will, "hate this world," meaning that we are assured of problems, heartaches, and troubles, and will surely suffer as foreigners in a strange place. Is this difficult teaching, coming directly from the mouth of Jesus, how the Christian life was explained to you in Sunday school? Does your church teach that you must die to yourself in order to live for Christ? — Probably not. Jesus' words offended many in His day, and they still offend today, which might be the reason many churches avoid Scripture.

Some of the largest churches in America teach that, once we become Christians, life is always good and that we will all prosper financially, live in good health, and live happily ever after; if this picture does not describe your life, then surely you are living in some sin, right? — Wrong! The misguided teachings of many churches stem from an ignorance of Jesus' teachings. Some churches avoid the Old Testament, including the book of Job (which directly contradicts the hurtful and ignorant teaching of the "prosperity gospel"). No wonder so many of us got so lost and gave up! Jesus never taught the "health and wealth" gospel, but rather the opposite. Jesus told us that, if we truly love Him and desire to serve Him, we will follow Him into suffering and death. Fortunately, Jesus does not stop there, but He goes on to say that we will also have Him with us, holding us, guiding us, helping us, loving us, and giving us peace through the storms, not IF they come, but WHEN they come. Jesus clearly told us that, "In this world you will have trouble, but I have overcome the world" (John 16:33). We are promised victory through life's pain in the end, and honor from God the Father.

The problem with much of our "Christian" teaching in the Church is the lack of Scriptural knowledge, the lack of Bible reading, and the false teachings often imparted to the congregation, as some church-goers (who think they are Christians) make it up as they go along... and of course you will get lost this way! Reading the Blueprint is essential if you want to avoid the confusion of being lost. The Bible is not some magical book that makes all of our problems go away, or even causes all of our problems to make sense; rather, it is a guide to help us get through those problems, and it helps us avoid self-inflicted problems as well. Most importantly, Scripture shows us the nature and character of God so that we can know Him. Without a firm grasp of Scripture, we cannot have the slightest idea who God is, but we form, and mold, and box Him into whatever and whoever we want Him to be.

God in a Box

So many "Christians" do not read their Bibles, and rely on their pastor, Sunday school teacher, or church to tell them who God is, what He expects, what is in the Bible, how to follow Christ and they claim the Christian faith. "That's what I've always been told," or "That's what my pastor said" are common phrases in the Church. What if your pastor does not read the Bible? What if he is passing along tradition he has been told, and the false teachings about God and His Word are simply perpetuated generation after generation? Scriptural ignorance is a problem within the Church and is more common than many people realize. "Study to show yourself approved" (II Timothy 2:15) is a verse apparently unknown to many.

Many continue to put God in a box of their own limited, impressionable minds, making Him who they want Him to be, who "works for them," and who makes them comfortable. Many often "create" God, the Creator, as some Being who loves us no matter what we do (which is true), but who also who accepts us no matter what we do, (which is not true). Some people, including those who call themselves "Christians," claim we place God in a box when we say that the only way to God, the Father, is through Jesus, the Son, and that such a view is a narrow-minded, boxed-in view of God. There is a major logical fallacy with this line of thinking for those who consider themselves Christians; again, this is due to ignorance regarding Scripture. Jesus Himself said, "No one comes to the Father except through Me" (John 14:6). If God is put in a box when we believe that Jesus is the only way to God, then it is Jesus Himself who put God in a box! Either you believe Scripture, or you do not; but, a Christian is a person who claims to believe the Bible as it is written, and not according to what they want it to say or think it says. Are you living in the addiction of ignorance and apathy, making up your faith and your god as you go along in life? Do you need recovery from this insanity and confusion?

The Old Testament book of Judges speaks about the horrible tragedies and violence of a generation of people who no longer knew God. Judges 21:25 says, "In those days there was no king in Israel; all the people did what was right in their own eyes." It seems as if, in our day, there is little knowledge of King Jesus, through Scripture, and the masses do what is right in their own eyes.

We need the Scriptures to guide us so that we can do what is right in the eyes of our King.

Recovery
Maybe you do not need to recover from alcoholism or drug addiction, but you do need to recover from the idolatry of creating the god of your own mind, your own golden calf, your attempt to stuff god in a box, your addiction to ignorance, and your self-imposed foolishness and hypocrisy. We all need recovery from the religion and god we created, which led us down so many wrong roads. Open your Bible and begin your recovery.

Alcoholics Anonymous has its Twelve Step program for addictions recovery, which has helped millions of people find sobriety and their "Higher Power," but not necessarily God and the Truth. In India, I began my own spiritual Twelve Step program, and my prayer is that, through the stories I told and the applications I made, these spiritual Twelve Steps may help you in your journey of self-recovery, and recovery in Jesus Christ:

Recovery is found through an intimate relationship with Jesus Christ. Jesus is known through a firm understanding of the Bible, which is the Blueprint for life and the basis of a Christian's beliefs, life, and eternity. May you find recovery and return to the self God intended in your journey through Scripture, and may you find a beautiful, holy, loving, merciful, forgiving, righteous Savior along the way.

With a life lived in love, according to Scripture, you will recover and return to the self God intended at your creation. The beautiful and poignant words of Dietrich Bonhoeffer sum it all up well; "Man's apostasy from Christ is at the same time his apostasy from his own essential nature" (Bonhoeffer, 110).

THE TWELVE STEPS

1. Admit that we all pretend and are hypocritical at times.
2. Acknowledge that you are lost.
3. Discover God through Jesus Christ.
4. Begin to develop a Christ-centered world view.
5. Learn to see God in daily life.
6. Deny yourself for the sake of loving others.
7. Allow Jesus to be more, and yourself to be less.
8. Learn to love, help, and live selflessly.
9. Understand your will as it conflicts with God's will.
10. Learn to trust, love, and obey God completely.
11. Understand safety as found in Scripture and in the center of God's will.
12. Recover yourself through Scripture.

"Peace to you brothers and sisters, and love with faith from God the Father and the Lord Jesus Christ. Grace to all who love our Lord Jesus Christ with an undying love."
(Ephesians 6:23)

REFERENCES

Bonhoeffer, Dietrich. *Ethics.* Collier Books, Macmillan Publishing Company, New York: 1963.

E.W. Bullinger. *A Critical Lexicon and Concordance to the English and Greek New Testament.* Kregel Publications, Grand Rapids, Michigan: 1999.

Mother Teresa: *No Greater Love.* New World Library, Novato, California: 1989.

The Companion Bible (The Authorized Version of the *King James Bible*, 1611). Ed., E.W. Bullinger, Kregel Publications, Grand Rapids, Michigan: 1922.

Twelve Steps and Twelve Traditions: Alcoholic Anonymous. World Services, Inc., New York, New York: 2008.

The New Oxford Annotated Bible. Edited by Bruce M. Metzger, University Press, New
York, New York: 1994.

VanHoozer, Kevin J. ed. *Dictionary for Theological Interpretation of the Bible.* Baker Academic, Grand Rapids, MI: 2005

Recovery: A Return to the Self
ISBN 978-1-935434-51-1
Donna Kasik

www.ingramcontent.com/pod-product-compliance
Lightning Source LLC
Chambersburg PA
CBHW071720090426

42738CB00009B/1826